GROW
ON THE
RAILWAY
IN THE
SOUTH WEST

GRACE HORSEMAN

ARK PUBLICATIONS (RAILWAYS)

First published in 1998 by ARK PUBLICATIONS (RAILWAYS), an imprint of Forest Publishing, Woodstock, Liverton, Newton Abbot, Devon TQ12 6JJ

British Library Cataloguing in Publication Data

A catalogue record for this book is available from the British Library

ISBN 1 873029 05 5

ARK PUBLICATIONS (RAILWAYS)

Editorial, layout and design by:
Grace Horseman and Mike Lang

Typeset by:
Carnaby Typesetting, Torquay, Devon TQ1 1EG

Printed and bound in Great Britain by:
The Latimer Trend Group, Plymouth, Devon PL6 7PL

Front cover illustration:

The arrival of a GWR 0–6–0 pannier tank locomotive and its train at a rural branch line station.

(Paul Hardy)

CONTENTS

DEDICATION

I should like to dedicate this book to my nephew and godson, David Shillito, because without his interest and encouragement it would never have been written. David knew that I had recently completed *Growing Up in the Forties* and might be at a loose end, so suggested a book about the railway in the area (where he was formerly an engineer) while some of the former GWR employees and others were still around.

My thanks are due to him for introducing me to some of the contributors, and also to the Reverend David Hardy and Douglas Croker for similar help. Finally, to everyone who has devoted time and trouble to write his (or her) experiences of the railway in the South West. I hope that their recollections will bring back happy memories to many other people.

PREFACE

A nostalgic love of the old steam locomotive still persists, although each year fewer and fewer remain of those who spent hours train-spotting when they were youngsters. Yet the force of these steam monsters also attracts the modern generation, as can be judged by the enthusiasm with which they enjoy a day out on the privately-run old branch lines such as those between Paignton and Kingswear, and Buckfastleigh and Totnes.

So I thought it appropriate to add a book on the railway in the South West to other *Growing Up* books that I have written. It includes personal reminiscences by former employees of the Great Western and other railway companies, and also from those who remember being passengers. In addition, I have introduced some more formal information, including mention of nationalisation and then the privatisation again in the 'nineties.

Many books have already been written containing much factual information about locomotives and the railway: I hope that this will give a more personal glimpse into life on the railway in the South West.

Grace Horseman
October 1998

INTRODUCTION

For more than 150 years thousands of people have 'grown up on the railway in the South West . Yet, until now, few books have been devoted exclusively to their personal experiences and memories, either as former employees or as passengers.

In the pages that follow are contributions from just a tiny proportion of these people, many having worked on the railway in jobs ranging from civil engineer to engine driver, from supervisor to porter, from signalman to office clerk, and so on – and in times dating back to before the Second World War. The oldest joined the Great Western Railway in 1917.

Since the Second World War the railway itself has undergone many changes, not only in the South West but over the country as a whole. First and foremost was that of nationalisation, when the four main companies that had operated the country's railway system since the Grouping of 1923 – the Great Western Railway (the only large railway company to have retained its identity at that time), the Southern Railway, the London, Midland and Scottish Railway, and the London and North Eastern Railway – were brought into State ownership. That was in 1948 and, in itself, had little meaning in the operating sense, although for many it was accompanied by great sadness: the Great Western Railway, which has evoked the most controversy, enthusiasm and nostalgia, was no more. 'God's Wonderful Railway', as it is now often affectionately called, had passed into history.

Another effect of nationalisation was that when economy measures were necessary – and this was, by then, already becoming a fact of life with ever-increasing private car ownership and with more and more freight being transported by road – the whole of the country's railway system was affected, rather than just part of it. Moreover, it was the rural areas, including those of the South West, that were most affected, for it was the more profitable urban and main lines that were soon receiving financial priority.

Further changes, which included the closure of many

5

The sea wall between Teignmouth and Dawlish has always been one of the most photogenic sections of railway line in the country. Depicted above is the Royal Train passing Teignmouth in 1902, with King Edward VII and Queen Alexandra on board after having visited Dartmouth and Plymouth.

Douglas Croker

secondary routes and branch lines as a means of tackling an ever-increasing annual running deficit, occurred during the modernisation programme of the 1950s and early 1960s. Then, in 1963, nearly the whole of the former Great Western Railway system in the West Midlands, the Borders and North Wales was transferred from the Western Region of British Railways to the London Midland Region. In exchange, part of the former Southern Railway system in the South West passed to Western Region, but within only a few more years many of these lines had also been lost by closure. In fact, apart from the main line from Waterloo to Exeter (and the section west of Coleford Junction (near Crediton) to Meldon Quarry, which was retained for the transportation of ballast), only the branches to Barnstaple, Exmouth and Gunnislake still survive.

In the meantime, the former Great Western Railway system in the South West was itself shrinking rapidly for similar reasons, one of the earliest casualties having been the Princetown branch, in 1956. Indeed, because of the cutbacks, combined with the transition from steam to diesel and electric traction during the 1960s, the railways changed almost beyond recognition and resulted in many of the links with the past being lost forever.

Over the years that followed, the railway system, in general, enjoyed a period of relative stability, and most of the changes made were simply to keep pace with progress, especially as regards locomotive and rolling stock design, and signalling. A particularly successful innovation to occur in the 1970s was that of Parkway stations, where motorists were encouraged to park their cars and continue their journeys by train; these were opened at Bristol, Tiverton and other locations so as to ease traffic congestion in certain towns and cities. However, in 1996, came another major change: the railways were privatised. Since then, trains on the main line to the South West from Paddington have been operated by Great Western Trains, using HST (High Speed Train) sets, whilst local services have been operated by Wales & West Passenger Trains, some of which are known as 'Alphaline' services. In addition, another company, South West Trains, now runs through services (mainly with 'turbo' diesel units) from Waterloo to Salisbury and Exeter, with a few trains continuing to Paignton, while Virgin Trains run through services, mostly with HST sets, to and from the Midlands and the North, from Penzance, via Bristol. At the same time, the

English, Welsh and Scottish Railway Company is responsible for the movement of all freight and mineral trains.

So, in effect, the wheel has almost turned full circle and we are back to private ownership, although the track and general infrastructure is now the responsibility of Railtrack, and the train operating companies do not own their trains but hire them from three other companies (known as ROSCO) set up at privatisation to take over the ownership of all the rolling stock. Only time will tell what the future holds.

Grace Horseman
October 1998

1. (a) CIVIL ENGINEER (b) MECHANICAL ENGINEER

(a) Mr Geoffrey P Mallett started work in May 1946 in the new works office of the chief (civil) engineer at Paddington as a surveyor/draughtsman. When he left the railway in 1955 he was a chartered civil engineer:–

In the winter of 1946 I attended a signalling class, which initiated me into the rules governing the safe operation of the railway. I had always had a proper respect for the responsibility carried by signalmen, and this was extended to the importance of all staff keeping to the rules. I was particularly proud to learn about the GWR automatic train control (ATC) and other 'fail-safe' checks in the system.

On 11 February 1947 I reported to the resident engineer at Greenford. The project was the extension of the London Transport Central Line from Greenford to West Ruislip and, although the Great Western Railway became British Railways (Western Region) on 1 January 1948, this made little change to my work.

With the conclusion of the Central Line contract, I was summoned to the chief engineer, Mr A. S. Quartermaine, to decide my future posting. The awe-inspiring corridor leading to his office ran at the roof level of Brunel's Paddington Station, and it contained paintings and photographs commemorating former chief engineers and their works. 'Q', as he was known, a past president of the Institution of Civil Engineers, skimmed over my file and offered me the options of either Wolverhampton or Taunton division – I chose Taunton and subsequently reported for duty there on 1 July 1949.

At first I was in 'digs' in Taunton and travelled home to Twickenham for the alternate weekends when I was not working on the Saturday morning. To enable me to return to Taunton on the Sunday, there was a train leaving Paddington mid-afternoon, but usually I would catch the 9.50pm with a colleague. We would play a game of pocket chess to pass the time and arrive at Bristol Temple Meads soon after midnight. There the train waited for an hour or so and took on board sailors returning from the North and the Midlands. By the time that we were on the move again everyone was dozing – although we were awakened by the clatter over the diamond crossing at Highbridge before arriving at Taunton at 2.40am. In addition to privilege tickets, there were free tickets for foreign travel. So I was able to visit the French Riviera and Milan, the Austrian Tyrol and Oberammergau, and the Bernese Oberland. We said that we could travel anywhere, but could hardly afford to leave the train!

In 1951 my folk moved to Cullompton and I came 'home' to them there. This then meant that I had to ride my bicycle to the station every morning in order to catch the 7.45am train to Taunton – sometimes it was a close-run thing! I also met several regular fellow travellers – one in particular, Margaret, has been with me ever since.

The divisional engineer was responsible for the maintenance and safety of the permanent way, bridges and other structures and buildings within his limits, which at that time included the main lines from Highbridge and Castle Cary to Totnes and the branch lines to Barnstaple (from Taunton), Chard, Minehead, Weymouth, Brixham, Kingswear (ferry to Dartmouth), Moretonhampstead and Hemyock, as well as the Exe Valley line. These were the old GWR lines, some destined for closure by the 1960s. In order to rationalise the boundaries of the nationalised Western and Southern Regions, the Western gave up the Weymouth and Chard branches and gained the Exeter to Barnstaple line along with others, since closed.

The divisional engineer had a deputy, a drawing office staff with a permanent way section, an accounts office, a general office and an engineering depot.

Ten permanent way inspectors were charged with the maintenance of some 1,400 miles of permanent way and the other railway property in their areas. Each ganger, or other authorised person, was required by Rule 221 to walk his length daily, attending to any loose keys or other fastenings and generally seeing that all was well. Annual work programmes proposed by the permanent way inspectors were vetted and finalised by the divisional engineer's staff so as to enable the DE to certify every year that all the lines for which he was responsible were safe.

During my short stint in the permanent way section I detailed the dimensions for relaying a crossover and improved the alignment of a length of track by averaging overlapping versines. Five young surveyors/draughtsmen were kept busy with a variety of tasks such as private sidings, canals, schemes and estimates for small works to bridges, station and depot buildings, goods sheds, loading bays and yards, improvements to staff amenities, levels, drainage, roof waterproofing etc, and there was a specialist dealing with agreements and easements. I also had my share of the variety and two stock programmes – repainting of buildings and maintenance of roadways and goods yards. Taunton concrete depot, incidentally, used to supply most of the precast concrete products used by the 'Western', including blocks, huts, fence posts, manhole units, signal and telegraph department items and prestressed concrete bridge beams.

My first job on the track in the South West was to measure up on a bridge near Hele and Bradninch Station. I was fairly relaxed about safety after having worked on electrified tracks – with new linen tapes rather than steel tapes and with trains every two minutes – and was quietly getting on with this work in the peace and quiet of the country. Suddenly came a call of "Look up!" There was the London express much too close for comfort, and my chainman and I had to move ourselves pretty quickly! Needless to say, I was considerably more careful on the tracks after that, where I became used to taking 26 short steps and then a little skip for the 27th when a joint was reached at every 60 feet: some of us fancied that we walked down the street like this, too!

Certain other jobs were also especially memorable. One was at Paignton Station, where bracing had to be added to the trestles of the footbridge so as to prevent it from swaying when large numbers of people from opposite ends met in the middle.

Then improvements were being made to Weymouth Quay that included the construction of a new cargo stage, work that had to be carried out in stages with occupations which could not exceed eight hours. In this instance, I prepared a scheme for relaying the tracks on precast concrete 'pads' with projecting reinforcement and in-situ concrete placed in subsequent occupations to form a continuous slab.

In Dainton tunnel, on the summit between Newton Abbot and Totnes, the drainage was not working adequately for the proper

Above: Weymouth Quay, where 0–6–0T No. 1370 is seen hauling 'The Wessex Wyvern', a Railway Correspondence & Travel Society sponsored rail tour, back towards the station on 8 July 1956.

Peter W. Gray

Below: Dainton tunnel, where 4–6–0 No. 6025 *King Henry III* is seen emerging from the western end with Ocean Mail coaches, c1960.

Mike Vinten

maintenance of the track. Sleepers were pumping in water which could not get away. As a result, quantities of shillet and, in one place, granite had to be broken with drills and removed so as to provide a sufficient gradient for new concrete drains. Key work required six weekend occupations, and work that could be done between trains was carried out on weekdays. Setting the levelling pegs was a tedious business between trains on weekdays. When a train came through with its banking engine, we retreated to a refuge for quite some time until the steam dispersed enough to see the levelling staff again. The weekend hours, meanwhile, were somewhat unsocial and did not always mean that good connections could be made with the train home. One chilly morning ride was on a tank engine travelling in reverse. A rather more comfortable ride was in a brake van which was kindly stopped for me at Cullompton.

Once all the drawing office staff were out on an emergency operation due to two 'King' class engines travelling close-coupled at excessive speeds between Taunton and Castle Cary. This had caused £10,000 worth of crippled rails which we had to identify and mark for replacement!

I also recall the 'whitewash trains' which recorded on a chart the rideability of the track, indicating where packing or other work was needed – in extreme cases by a splash of whitewash to indicate the need for attention by the P.W. gang concerned. The Hallade recorder comprised three pendulums mounted at right angles. Each pendulum was linked to a pen scribing on a paper chart at a constant speed of 1 mm/sec. We made clicks as we passed lineside objects and, in particular, we clicked each $1/4$, $1/2$, $3/4$ and 1 mile-post on Line 1. On Line 2 we marked the curvature, LH or RH; Line 3 showed longitudinal vibrations; Line 4 transverse vibrations (alignment); and Line 5 vertical vibrations (packing). The speed of the run at any point could be checked quickly from the spacing of the milepost ticks, using the special Hallade Scale.

To complete my training as a civil engineer, I was given the opportunity, in 1952, of a temporary transfer for nine weeks to the bridge office at Paddington for the purpose of designing a small prestressed concrete bridge. Prestressed concrete was then a comparatively new technique, pioneered in France and Belgium and taken up by BR's Eastern and Western Regions. I prepared calculations, drawings and the bill of quantities and, after returning to Taunton, I was able to visit the concrete depot to see

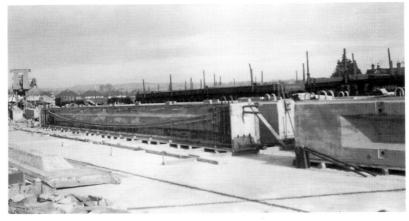

Ten prestressed concrete bridge beams being cast at Taunton concrete depot in 1952.

Above: Post-tensioning five tendons in each beam. Jacking force 33 tons each tendon.

Left: Testing a beam with two 10-ton loads at midspan (representing 50% overload), checking deflection.

the beams being manufactured and tested. In 1953 I was transferred back to the new works office and on Saturday/Sunday 19/20 September I saw my beams installed at Saltney, near Chester.

After a spell of fieldwork (with myxomatous rabbits) on the development of the station and sidings at Goodrington, it was time for a career move to different work. Nevertheless, I left the 'Western' in March 1955 with mixed feelings: whilst looking forward to a change of work, I had enjoyed my time and met some

Above left: Placing an outside beam in position at Saltney, near Chester, on Sunday, 20 September 1953. *Above right:* All beams placed and transversely stressed together, and the track relaid by 4.45pm, leaving the remainder of parapet units, posts and handrails to be fixed between trains on the following Monday.

All five photographs G. P. Mallett

A steam crane lowering pre-stressed concrete beams (cast at Taunton concrete depot) to form the then new Tanner's Road bridge at Goodrington on 4 December 1955. In attendance, underneath the new bridge, is Newton Abbot-based 2–8–0 No. 2809, while just off picture (to the right) is 4–6–0 No. 6829 *Burmington Grange.*

Peter W. Gray

15

great characters, not least the chainmen – salts of the earth! My time had also spanned some of the last days of steam, and the structure of the 'Western', even after nationalisation, was not that different from that of the GWR. Little did we know how much things would change! It is ironic almost 50 years on to hear suggestions of getting some of the goods off the roads and onto the railways!

(b) David Shillito, C Eng. MI Mech E B Sc Hons. was born in Northern Rhodesia in May 1948 and moved with his family to England in 1963. Upon completing his secondary education at Rutlish School in South Merton, Surrey, and an A-level course at Churston Ferrers Grammar School in Devon, he moved to Plymouth Polytechnic to specialise in mechanical engineering and is currently employed by the English Welsh and Scottish Railway Company, based at Toton depot, near Nottingham:–

My first introduction to British Railways occurred in February 1963, when I arrived in England with my family – fresh (and frozen) off the ship at Southampton. The train that hauled us up to London was headed by a steam locomotive, and the coaches were steam-heated as was evident from steam rising out from under the seats: the damp burnt-coal smell of that coach is still embedded in my memory.

Upon leaving school and moving to Plymouth in order to begin my mechanical engineering course, I was advised that I would have to undertake four six-month-long sessions of industrial training and that it was my responsibility to secure places with suitable companies. Having researched the local and national engineering-related companies, I then decided that British Railways offered the most varied and interesting engineering training and duly applied for my first six-month training session. After an interview in the North Road Station offices at Plymouth, with the divisional locomotive engineer from Bristol and the depot engineer from Plymouth, I was accepted for six months industrial training at Laira depot which, by then, was the main Western Region depot for the diesel hydraulic Western class and Warship class locomotives.

At Laira depot I was placed with the locomotive inspectors. When a locomotive came in for maintenance an 'initial work' inspector would examine it from top to bottom and book every defect found. Later, the 'final work' inspector would examine and test the locomotive to ensure that all the required work had been done and that it was safe to return to service. These inspectors did most of the fault-finding at the depot and most of the riding of locomotives in service so as to ensure that they were working correctly.

The D800, D803 and D866 series of Warship diesel hydraulic locomotives were built by British Railways at their Swindon works and were fitted with two German turbocharged Maybach engines which drove two axles mounted on each bogie through a Mekydro transmission: the bogie is the frame which holds the locomotive axles and allows the locomotive to pass around curves in the track by rotating under the locomotive main frame. In these diesel hydraulic locomotives the engine to gearbox, and gearbox to axle final-drive units, were connected by cardan shafts to transmit the engine power to the wheels. The Mekydro gearboxes changed gear automatically by emptying and filling a torque converter with oil so as to allow the sliding dogs within the gearbox to engage mechanically each gear in turn.

One of my early tasks as a trainee was to jump on each Warship class locomotive as it arrived at Laira, lift up the cab floor and apply strips of heat sensitive paint to the gearbox oil heat-exchanger pipes from the torque converter. I then had to examine the colour of each strip of paint on each locomotive and record the findings over a three-month period. As a result of these tests it was found that the hydraulic control unit in each gearbox had to be adjusted to ensure that the correct fill and emptying time for the torque converters at each end of the locomotive were synchronised with each other and with the gear change sequence so as to prevent the oil from overheating. Each gearbox was the size of an Austin Mini and was very hot.

I accompanied the inspectors on in-service rides on these Warship locomotives from Plymouth to Penzance and to Taunton. It was fascinating seeing how these 1,100 horsepower engines operated – the heat; the noise; the smell; the bright red exhaust pipes feeding into the single turbocharger; the engine governor controlling the engine speed and power; the clunk and bang of each gear change; and the synchronising of each gearbox to ensure that gear changes at each end did not occur at the same time – and thereby cause the passengers behind to spill their coffee or tea!

On one such trip we had two Warships in multiple pulling Harold Wilson's train down to Penzance. This time there were four engines and four gearboxes to attend to!

The train carriages were still heated by steam. The steam generator was carried in the middle of the locomotive between the two engines and burned diesel oil to convert the water into steam. This was then piped down the train in much the same manner as in the days of steam locomotives.

The Western diesel hydraulic locomotives, which were built by British Railways at their Swindon and Crewe works, again had two Maybach engines, but were fitted with a Voith Turbo transmission driving three axles on each bogie. This transmission changed gear by filling and emptying three converters in conjunction with gear ratios to drive the final-drive cardan shaft. The steam generator for train heating was again located between the two engines.

After my first five months at Laira helping the depot staff to maintain, fault-find, repair and ride these locomotives, my next assignment was to spend some time with the stores supervisor, learning how 'A' and 'B' stock stores items were controlled and ordered. 'A' stock was the more expensive one-off items such as dynostarters, bogies, wheelsets, gearboxes, transmissions, engines, cardan shafts, steam generators, drivers' seats, gauges etc., and they were ordered individually from the main stores in Swindon works. The 'B' stock items, cheaper multi-use items such as pins, nuts, bolts, washers, again came from Swindon works, but were ordered in bulk when a predetermined number remained in the stores bin.

Subsequent industrial training periods were again spent with the chief mechanical and electrical engineer (CM & EE) of British Railways (Western Region), as I had accepted their offer of sponsorship and future employment. The second and third six-month sessions, however, were spent at Swindon works, initially in the apprentice training school, and then in the main works seeing how they manufactured as many of the 'B' stock items as was possible and how 'A' stock items were manufactured or repaired. I spent time in the spring shop making the large 12-inch diameter suspension coil springs; in the pattern shop and foundry, casting brake valves and other ferrous and non-ferrous components; in the engine overhaul shop, where the twelve-cylinder turbocharged and intercooled Maybach engines were reconditioned; and in the transmission, bogie and wheelset shops. The final few weeks were spent in the locomotive assembly shops, where all the parts came together to form a Western diesel hydraulic locomotive.

The fourth and final training period was spent in Bristol with the plant engineer, overhauling Plassermatic track maintenance machines and other items of plant; and at Laira with the depot engineer seeing how locomotive availability and reliability was monitored and controlled; and how staff bonus payments were calculated, based on work done.

After graduating in 1973, I was posted to Western Region headquarters at Paddington to assist the locomotive engineers in experiments and modifications to improve locomotive performance; with maintenance and shopping control; and with casualty investigations on the 08 shunters and classes 25, 35, 37, 46, 47 and 52 locomotives. The classes 37, 46 and 47 locomotives and the 08 shunters were diesel-electric locomotives, and much of my time was spent on electrical problem solving. With the arrival of the class 50 electronic control electric locomotives on the Western Region, I also spent some time at the newly formed electronic repair centre and school before being returned to Laira depot in 1974 as the casualty investigator responsible for the monitoring and solving of the electrical and electronic problems on our allocation of locomotives, primarily on the class 50. Simply put, the diesel-electric locomotive has a diesel engine which drives a generator, which supplies controlled electric current to its traction motors, each of which drives an axle. By this time the diesel-electric locomotives had started working on the Western Region, and classes 37, 45, 46, 47 and 50 locomotives visited the depot. Some English Electric engined classes 37, 46 and 50 locomotives were allocated to Laira depot for maintenance.

The class 50 locomotive was the production version of the prototype 2,700 horsepower English Electric DP2 locomotive and it was fitted with the newly developed chopper thyristor electronic control 'KV10' circuitry for power control. Other electronic circuits controlled the chopper thyristors, the engine radiator fan, the electric train-heat generator, battery charging, the field diversion for 'gear changing' and the dynamic (rheostatic) brake.

I spent a lot of my time working on the class 50 locomotives to improve their reliability and availability. By 1976 the last of the diesel hydraulic main line locomotives were being scrapped and were being replaced by the class 50 locomotives. Having made up test-boxes to monitor the performance of the electronic control units in service, it was found that the majority of failures were due to fatigue failure of the small electronic component mountings and associated wires.

Western diesel-hydraulic locomotive No. D1023, one of the last operational locomotives of its class to haul British Railway trains, outside the now-demolished servicing shed at Laira depot in 1977.
David Shillito

The dynamic brake on the class 50 locomotive was efficient when it worked, but drivers did not like it as the braking current generated by the traction motors, now acting as generators, was shown as a reading on the drivers' main traction current gauge. Some drivers isolated the dynamic brake to avoid this conflict, but depot tests took eight hours to reinstate the dynamic brake, which resulted in loss of availability of locomotives. The traction motors and main generators were also prone to earth faults. The need to remove the dynamic brake, to carry out modifications, and the need to rewire and remove redundant equipment, resulted in the class 50 locomotives undergoing a refurbishment programme at Doncaster works from 1979 onwards.

Whilst at Laira I had the chance to go out with the breakdown gang to re-rail vehicles in the South West. Laira had a 45-ton steam crane which was used to re-rail wagons, coaches and locomotives. One outing of the breakdown team was to St Dennis, in Cornwall, in order to recover two 00V china clay tip wagons which had been allowed to run down the hill into the stop blocks that marked the closure of the St Dennis to Newquay branch line. The wagons had hit the stop blocks and then proceeded over them before rolling over onto their sides. With the crane on the front of a Western hydraulic locomotive, we slowly moved down the hill to recover the first wagon from the stop blocks. The second wagon was left as the crane could not reach it.

Other Western Region traction maintenance depots that I visited were located at Newton Abbot, Bristol, Cardiff, Swansea and Old Oak Common. Smaller depots were at Penzance, St Blazey, Exeter, Swindon, Oxford, Worcester, Gloucester and Reading.

With the decision taken in 1979 to refurbish the class 50 locomotives, I was relocated to the Western Region headquarters in Paddington to project manage their refurbishment on behalf of the CM& EE Western Region. However, in 1986 I returned to Laira and then moved down to St Blazey in order to look after all freight activities in the South West, especially the movement of china clay. Whilst there, I was also involved in the refurbishment of the depot to BS5750 standard, part of which included the provision of drainage and oil interception of an extended car parking area. Furthermore, it was decided that a 'centre-piece' should be positioned in the car park so as to demonstrate the involvement of St Blazey depot in the china clay industry, and that this 'centre-piece' would be an OOV china clay (clay-hood) wagon. It would all depend, though, on such a wagon being located as the fleet of OOV wagons had since been replaced (in 1988) by 125 CDA wagons and those that had not been sold to preservation societies had been scrapped. In addition, the stock of the blue hoods had been sold to a pig farmer in the north of England.

As a result, I first of all went down to St Dennis to see if the wagon abandoned behind the stop blocks on the closed St Dennis to Newquay branch line was still there. Although this proved to be futile (only a few fragments of the wagon could be found), I then remembered a request being made from a railway preservation society in 1989 for permission to remove parts from a damaged clay-hood wagon at Coombe Junction and stopped off on my return from Laira depot. This wagon, which had run away from Moorswater Clay Works in 1986 and become derailed, was still there, hidden in the undergrowth.

As B743835 had a bent axle and frame, my colleagues and I decided that we could jack up the wagon onto rollers to re-rail it onto the Coombe Junction to Moorswater line. Then, once the

The 00V china clay wagon left at Coombe Junction, near Liskeard, after derailment on 20 October 1986.

David Shillito

The 00V china clay wagon being restored at St Blazey in 1993. Here, Vernon Armstrong is applying a chalk line before painting on wagon data.

David Shillito

wagon was on the track, we could fit a wheel-skate under the bent axle and use a locomotive to pull it to Moorswater Clay Works, prior to being loaded onto a lorry and transported to St Blazey.

At St Blazey depot the only remaining member of staff in 1993 to have the knowledge and experience to rebuild completely a clay-hood wagon was Jim Perryman, who immediately set about organising the necessary work programme. The wagon was then stripped of all its old wood; the metal work was shotblasted, primed and painted; and the bent axle was sent off to a local engineering firm to be straightened. Meanwhile, new wood was located at the now closed Motherwell wagon depot in Glasgow and delivered to St Blazey, using the delivery service provided by the Railway National Supply Centre.

Soon, Jim had straightened as much metal work as was possible and rebuilt the wagon. A spare blue hood was kindly provided by a member of staff, who had purchased one to cover his car, and, on 27 August 1993 (the day of Jim's retirement after 49 years service), the completed wagon was lifted off the track outside St Blazey

The 00V china clay wagon, now fully restored and in its place of honour at St Blazey, 1993.

David Shillito

wagon shops and ceremoniously placed on a plinth. A brass plaque was also mounted on a granite rock recovered from the china clay quarry at Goonbarrow, and this reads:–

OOV Clay Wagon 743835
This wagon was restored by
Jim Perryman
and his colleagues
at St. Blazey
and sited here on
27th August 1993
as a memorial to
staff past, present and future.

Note: Wagon B743835 must not be used unless the straightened bent axle is replaced.

Apart from becoming involved in such an interesting project as this, my move to St Blazey also enabled me to get re-acquainted with some of the people with whom I had worked in previous years. Many, though, had retired, and gone for ever is the unique experience that all these talented men and women had developed during their railway careers – the St Blazey blacksmith, the chargehand, the supervisor, the oiler, the railman, the shunter, the driver, the TOPS clerk and many more based throughout the South West.

Some have kindly contributed their own stories to this book by Grace Horseman, my dear aunt and godmother, and we keep in touch and help each other whenever we can. The railway family, although changed, does still exist!

(In 1992 St Blazey had come under the control of Railfreight Distribution, a subsidiary of British Railways, but in 1994 parts of the freight network were split up into freight companies and St Blazey was transferred to Transrail Limited. Then, in 1996, Wisconsin Central (in the United States) purchased the freight companies and formed EWS – English Welsh and Scottish Railway Company – and I am now employed by them as their vehicle acceptance and standards engineer, based at Toton TMD, near Nottingham.)

✳✳✳✳✳

2. SUPERVISOR/ AREA MAINTENANCE

During fifty years at Southern Railway's Exmouth Junction depot, Mr G. W. (Bill) Batten gained an excellent knowledge of the many functions carried out there:—

As a schoolboy I often visited Exmouth Junction depot and was so impressed by the work carried out in this Southern Railway complex that on 16 July 1942 (my big day!) I joined the railway at the age of fifteen. By then I had already completed two years' study at the Exeter Technical School of Engineering.

My last weeks at school were severely disrupted by heavy air raids on Exeter: 4 May was the worst. School was closed for several days, and when I returned it was difficult to come to terms with all the destruction and upheaval. Damaged classrooms had temporary repairs; all the windows were boarded up as the glass had been shattered; each road and street on the way to school carried the scars of bomb damage; and some classmates had lost their homes. School life was over: I felt the need to contribute to the world of work and became employed at Exmouth Junction locomotive depot as a fitter's lad until I could begin a five-year apprenticeship on my 16th birthday, in February 1943. This I found very exciting and friendly: I was free to explore many aspects of the new challenge.

Before the apprenticeship contract was signed I had to pass medical and eyesight tests. The medical examination went well, and the doctor was very thorough and understanding to a fifteen year old, but the eyesight examination was very different! This took place in the home of an eminent eye specialist in Exeter, where the examination and consulting rooms boasted the very best and latest equipment. Arriving on time at the front door of the very large house in elegant surroundings, I was greeted by a large elderly lady dressed in a long black skirt and a blouse with a high-necked collar, very Victorian in style. She said, in no uncertain

25

tone: "The entrance for railwaymen, tradesmen and little boys is by the *back* door". Lesson No. 1, in life always try to get the entrance right.

Exmouth Junction depot was sited on a very large area of land beside the main Southern line from London (Waterloo) to Exeter, where the branch line to Exmouth departs. At the time it was the most modern railway depot in the South West, if not in the whole country, with almost all the buildings made of reinforced concrete produced at the Exmouth Junction concrete works, part of the complex. Panel sections were held together by interlocking posts, and these, too, were of reinforced concrete made at the Exmouth Junction concrete works. Many of the installations made in the late 1920s, when Exmouth Junction was modernised, are still in use today. A fine example is the two footbridges that span the tracks at Exeter Central Station; one from the booking hall on the main line 'downside' to the 'upside' platform, the other at the London end of the station, with its entrance from New North Road, spanning the four tracks and giving access to the whole station. The extended 'upside' platform was made from prefabricated reinforced section supports with interlocking concrete slabs – the perfect platform. The lighting columns and signal gantries are other features made at the Exmouth Junction concrete department workshops.

The marshalling yard at Exmouth Junction enabled all materials for the numerous railway activities to be brought in from any place on the network and, similarly, the finished products to be transported out. Indeed, most of the freight from Southern Railway west of Exeter passed through Exmouth Junction marshalling yard. This included fresh vegetables and flowers from Cornwall and various dairy products, in particular thousands of gallons of milk from all over the region. In addition, because all of the ballast for the whole of the Southern Railway came from Meldon Quarry (near Okehampton), this also went through Exmouth Junction.

With this vast amount of traffic an excellent carriage and wagon maintenance and repair workshop was essential. Every vehicle that entered the workshop was examined and listed for maintenance/repairs. These went through the numerous sections from replacing a safety chain to the wheels being removed, the latter to be reprofiled in the lathe and then refitted with new bearings prior to being put back on the vehicle for a further working period – subject to a final examination before leaving the workshop. Older-type carriages were often stripped of seating and converted into mobile workshops for testing equipment when the Southern Railway was nationalised in 1948 and became part of British Rail.

Although looking after steam locomotives was hard and heavy work, we still found time for laughs, fun and general pranks. Whitewash was used a great deal in the depot and was easy to obtain. As most of the staff had bicycles we whitewashed these and hung them out to dry on any pretence to celebrate. The older men were very set in their ways, starting and finishing each day with clockwork timing, and this made it very easy for apprentices and fitters' lads to play pranks on them. As a result, they were often delayed when leaving work and this, in turn, made them arrive late at the pub before going home – a cardinal sin to the social life of the day. Several glasses of ale or cider were drunk to steady the nerves, and it was also an opportunity to meet the other workers from all walks of life in order to talk about local and national topics: they put the world to rights before the age of television! Most free time from work was spent in the pub.

The Exmouth Junction stores were the equivalent of today's hypermarket. They had to meet the requirements of such varied works as signal and telegraph, gas and water, carpenters' workshops and the many outstation, smaller workshops which stretched from Salisbury to Plymouth, from Exeter to Bude, and northwards to Ilfracombe.

Items required had to be placed on an order document and then collected at the check-out before being transported to the work area required by one of the many types of transporters available. These varied from battery-operated trucks, similar to today's milk floats, to smallish fork-lift trucks with hand-operated hydraulic pump systems, or were merely sack trucks and wheelbarrows. Restocking the stores was done 90% by rail, wagons from suppliers all over the country being shunted via the marshalling yard to an area known as the dock wall. This was a large platform section located at the same height as the wagon floor, making the off-loading of materials very easy. Overhead the rail track and unloading platform was a gantry with a hoist lift for the much heavier components such as side springs and wheel sets. All items were then taken by storemen to fill the shelves, racks or compounds set out for each component.

Many clerical staff were needed for the documentation procedures – there was no computer technology in those days!

Every item was ordered handwritten, always at least in duplicate, often in triplicate, and, sometimes, in the case of the more important and expensive items, in quadruple forms. Next to the office in which the clerks worked was an area known to all as 'Fort Knox', in which all the pens, ink, pencils, paper forms and other stock deemed high risk were kept.

The outdoor machinery department (always referred to as the ODM) had a large workshop at Exmouth Junction. Its main function was to maintain most of the ancillary equipment at Exmouth Junction and the many satellite depots in the area – Templecombe, Yeovil Junction, Lyme Regis, Sidmouth, Seaton Junction, Exmouth, Barnstaple, Wadebridge, Okehampton and Meldon Quarry. Each of these had a selection of water pumps, compressors, filtration equipment, lifting appliances and lathes of all sizes.

Until the late 1950s all travelling by ODM staff to the outstations was done by train. As many pieces of plant were at the trackside between stations, a special stop order had to be obtained from the train-operating manager to stop there, and on the return journey. This kind of maintenance, with little or no protection from the weather and no facilities to wash or prepare a hot drink and food, made very special demands on the employee.

Building and bridge department workshops were also part of the Exmouth Junction complex. Bridges were usually examined during the working week and repair/maintenance carried out at weekends, mostly at night so as to cause minimum interference to normal train traffic, which, in any event, was always less at weekends. Many coaches and wagons for this bridge work were adapted within Exmouth Junction carriage and wagon workshops, with supervisors from each department explaining the needs of one against another to gain the best results.

The locomotive shed at Exmouth Junction was very well designed and constructed, giving the best working conditions in the country before the Second World War. There were twelve shed roads for normal maintenance repairs and one with an overhead travelling and transversing crane to lift locomotives for wheel removal and major repairs. At the end was a large lathe for axle and wheel turning.

Each road length was capable of holding four of the longer type locomotives over full-length inspection pits. There was a good working area between each road and a well finished surface that benefitted from good drainage and was easy to keep clean. The roof gave excellent protection and also allowed natural light into what was a very large building. Above each track in the shed were smoke channels connected to chimney stacks which vented most of the steam and smoke, thus keeping the working environment acceptable. Outside, at the approach to each of the twelve shed roads, was an inspection pit suitable for the longest locomotives in service. Standing between these outside pits were water columns (each capable of providing a discharge rate of approximately 200 gallons per minute) for filling locomotive tenders and side tanks.

The depot water supply came from a storage tank with a 30,000-gallon capacity. This was set on a steel girder framework about 80 feet high, above a recycle filtration plant. The layout of the depot allowed all surplus and waste water to drain into the filtration chamber, where each section was packed with bales of woodwool at various levels. After passing through these, and being cleaned and softened with water briquettes as the final stage of purification, the water was then pumped to the storage tank for future use, at the same time keeping the amount of mains water required at the depot to a minimum.

The greatest amount of water used was that required for boiler washing, which was based on a very strict schedule according to the working hours of each locomotive. First the fire and ashes were removed from the firebox so as to allow the water within the boiler to cool, a process that took several hours. Then screw-type plugs were removed for the purpose of allowing the water to empty from the boiler. Finally, there were oval inspection plates at strategic points on the boiler case that had to be removed so that the boiler interior could be flushed with hose jets, thus removing any impurities that had built up since the previous wash out. This, in itself, was very important as occasionally contaminated water would carry impurities and excess water into the cylinders when heated, causing considerable damage.

When the task had been completed, the boiler inspector examined the boiler and his report for any repair/maintenance work was passed to the boilersmiths. Their work often included renewing the tubes, which carried the firebox heat through the boiler to the smokebox, or renewing the stays, which kept the firebox and boiler as one unit. Sometimes leaking stays were caulked by boilersmiths, but this work was extremely noisy and left many workers with hearing defects.

Coal, of course, was an essential, and this was brought from the mines to the depot by rail, mostly in wagons of 20-ton capacity. After coming through the marshalling yard, these were placed on a track beside the coal hopper, which was a reinforced structure about 70 feet high and capable of holding hundreds of tons of coal. Each wagon, in turn, was then moved by rope and capstan onto a platform lift, where it became locked into a frame, and hoisted some 40 feet before being rotated so as to allow the coal to fall into the hopper. Afterwards, the now empty wagon was returned to ground level, unlocked and moved off the platform so as to make way for the next loaded wagon. Keeping the hopper fairly full, incidentally, meant a reduced fall and a minimum amount of crushed coal, which was important as coal in lumps burned better than coal dust.

On its opposite side the coal hopper had discharge shutes above the track and at a height sufficient to allow a locomotive to pass under them. With the bunker, or tender, of the locomotive in position, the discharge shute door would then be opened and the required amount of coal released. Sometimes, however, a malfunction caused overfill and spillage, which had to be cleared into empty wagons manually. Needless to say, this was extremely hard and dirty work, and on windy days it was not unknown for coal dust to be blown all over the depot.

When a locomotive was being restocked with coal the firebox would be cleaned of surplus ashes and clinker that had gathered on the firebars and ashpan. It would then be moved onto the turntable to face the correct direction for the next duty required and given a berth in the shed, where an inspection was made by the mechanical staff.

In order to improve our knowledge of the working of steam locomotives, classes at the depot were arranged by senior management and inspectors. First Aid classes were also held at the depot, with teams competing against other depots and regions. The Exmouth Junction First Aid team won many cups and trophies in the UK and Europe. Another activity started at Exmouth Junction was the brass band. For many seasons it entertained the crowds at Exeter City football ground, at St James' Park, with superb music. Although they are not playing at football matches nowadays, the British Rail Brass Band is still going strong, with wonderful concerts being given in the area.

As was the custom, the final year of my apprenticeship was

completed at the main works of the Southern Railway at Eastleigh, in Hampshire: lodgings were found for me in the town, not far from the main entrance to the works. This was very different from Exmouth Junction, which was a 'running shed' working each day on many types and parts, for at the main works in Eastleigh just one aspect of a locomotive was worked on for days, if not weeks. Most weekends I was thrilled to travel from Eastleigh to Exeter, and back, by rail; and the enjoyment of rail travel has stayed with me all of my life.

I returned to Exmouth Junction as a fitter in 1948, when I had completed my apprenticeship; another chapter in my railway career had begun. Responsibility to the job in question now became of paramount importance. Also, after five years of daytime work from 7.30am to 5.00pm, I was now faced with shift work: a 6.00am start one week followed by 2.00pm to 10.00pm, and then 10.00pm to 6.00am, shifts was a shock to the system and meant a big adjustment to my social life. On the plus side, though, was the improvement in my means of transport – a motorbike in place of a bicycle!

It was accepted policy that relief work at the many satellite depots of Exmouth Junction for locomotive maintenance was carried out by the junior fitters. Consequently, during 1948 and 1949 I had to spend time at such varied locations as Templecombe, Yeovil, Barnstaple, Okehampton and my favourite, Wadebridge, a good depot and an outstanding place.

The mid-1950s saw staffing levels for the depot reach almost correct proportions for the first time since the end of the Second World War, and promotion to chargehand fitter not only gave me a new view on work but also made the following years slip by with comparative ease. However, there was a dramatic change in store for all railway staff when diesel locomotive power was introduced. In fact, many found it to be a disaster, unable to adapt after several years with steam, despite retraining courses. As a result, several employees left the railway, particularly the older element, while others moved into other departments of British Rail not connected with locomotive maintenance. The rest, however, soon started to enjoy this then new type of locomotive work, and I found myself being promoted to relief supervisor.

With the diesel locomotive being so versatile and maintenance patterns altering, the following years saw many old steam depots being closed. Eventually, Exmouth Junction became a victim, but I

Two photographs taken at Exmouth Junction, showing:–
Above: Unrebuilt 'Westcountry' class Pacific No. 34023 *Blackmore Vale* on 27 May 1961.

Mike Vinten

Below: BR standard class 4 2–6–4T No. 80043 standing in front of the steam shed on 2 October 1965.

Mike Vinten

was able to fill a vacancy at the road motor section Exeter depot and this kept me with the railway, maintaining smaller type diesel engines.

When the 'on track machine' maintenance was transferred from 'road motors' to 'outdoor machinery' section, which had workshops on the Exmouth Junction site, I returned to another phase of railway life. The effect of the ontrack machine to rail track maintenance was outstanding: more mileage maintained at a very high standard, with less manpower per shift, increased an area workload as far afield as Swindon, Gloucester, Bristol, Plymouth and Penzance. This enlarged my knowledge of the area, making nearly every workday a wonderful experience in a new venue.

With so many railway factors having changed over the 1970s and 1980s, maintenance of the many various types of work in the Exeter area became controlled by one supervisor. However, when a programme commenced to develop the Exeter St David's locomotive depot and that of St Blazey depot in Cornwall (to meet the requirements of the area under the control of the area fleet manager Plymouth (Laira)), another supervisor for each depot was appointed. I was the successful applicant for the post of area fleet manager Exeter, so involvement in rebuilding part of an industry that had occupied all my working life, 1942 to 1992, gave me a very memorable career.

Mr Mike Vinten shares his long fascination with the railway, first as an observer, then as a railway employee eventually to his present position as the area maintenance supervisor for Wales & West passenger trains:–

My love-hate relationship with railways began in 1942 when I was aged three. In those days weekly shopping trips by bus from Laleham (where I lived) to Staines was a highlight, and to see the old '2NOL' electric units, with some real steam age character about them, clattering by above the fish stall in the High Street was really something. The fish stall is still there, but the 2NOLs and restaurant, where Mum and I went for hot blackcurrant drinks, have long since gone.

Later, at about the time my sister was born in 1943, we lived with an aunt for a while. Her house was by the LMS main line, and a change of trains at Willesden High Level on the journeys that we made, with the sound and sight of heavy wartime goods trains leaning to the curve through the old semi-covered station on the North London line, was a really frightening thrill, especially when the safety valves opened with a sudden roar.

My aunt's house backed on to the main line south of Bushy water troughs, and my uncle's allotment, where we often played, was right on the cutting side. I can now only look back and imagine the sights and sounds of those hectic wartime days. I can't remember being frightened by the war, although the family suffered numerous casualties and house moves over the period. My dad was in the RAF, working with radar, and spent a lot of time in East Anglia. Mum, baby sister and I used to visit him, which led to many railway trips. I remember one engine working trains between Yarmouth and Lowestoft, which I firmly believe had only one buffer. If so, it shows the state that the country was in at that time. It must have been an 'auto' push-pull train, so the locomotive didn't need to change ends.

Whilst in this area I can also remember sitting in my pushchair (I had badly scalded my legs and feet when a kettle of boiling water fell off the living room fire, the gas being off) for a very long time outside a grocer's shop, when a barrage balloon came to earth in a ball of fire. My dad had forgotten he had taken me out that day! I don't remember the rain, but I was told that it was a thunderstorm that had ignited the balloon.

Towards the end of the war my family moved to Paignton, which, of course, meant more rail travel. Once we were out in the countryside, nature enthralled me. We still travelled back to Staines a couple of times each year, but it was now the birds, bees, trees and streams that absorbed all my energies.

After starting school a young gang of us spent much of the time raking around the fields, orchards, barns, woods and forests (the imagination running wild) scrumping gooseberries, raspberries, apples and, of course, blackberries, according to the time of year. When food was short a mangel-wurzel made a feast fit for a king in our young eyes. Making dams and bridges across streams, and camps were other favourite pastimes. As long as we were covered with red Devon mud, we were happy.

Towards the end of my time in junior school, my interest in railways reasserted itself and, whenever possible, I managed to get near the line. Once I had moved to school in Totnes, a number of us got together and made forays to Newton Abbot, Plymouth and Exeter, eventually visiting the locomotive depots, of which there were five in these three towns. These visits were quite unofficial, but we usually got by with a nod and wink from an amused railwayman.

By the time that I was fifteen and GCE's were approaching I hadn't a clue what I wanted to do. I wasn't over-keen at school and, although I was often top of the class in four or more subjects at the Christmas exams, I had usually slipped back quite a bit by the summer exams. I like to blame it on long absences that I had due to asthma, which was always worse from December onwards once colds were about, and then, with the coming of spring, the pollen really had me wheezing.

Surprisingly (or so it seemed then) I was always much improved on railway trip days, so people said it was psychological, as when I was doing something that I liked I was OK! But looking back I see that cold, dust, pollen and animals (cats, dogs and horses), the main 'triggers', were absent on the railway. So it seemed logical to find an interesting job on the railway, and what better place than Swindon – the great Mecca of the steam locomotive to us lads. Following a letter, interview and medical, I became an apprentice fitter turner and erector, starting at the end of 1955 in the 'B' shed at Swindon works.

At that time fitter apprentices there began work on the complete

A group of apprentices at Swindon, with Mike Vinten first on the left, posing for the camera on freshly turned-out 4–6–0 No. 6876 *Kingsland Grange*, c1957.

Mike Vinten

35

overhaul of loco tenders. Although this was not very complex, it provided a good grounding, especially as it involved working in a team with two other fitters – for the grand sum of £2.10.0d per week (plus a bonus, which certainly helped). It's now hard to believe that we managed let alone lived on that wage, but that was before inflation.

Every three months or so apprentices moved on to another operation so as to get them used to different types of work and to become better acquainted with the works. They learned the skills of turning, bench fitting, mill wrighting, tool making and, finally, locomotive erecting. Not all of the lads went to each gang, but all of them had similar work processes to complete. After work, night school took up a great part of the evenings throughout the year. However, we did manage to fit in a social life as well, and got home at weekends.

Soon after arriving, a group of likeminded lads organised weekend trips all over the country, visiting railway installations and depots, so we soon knew our geography pretty well.

An Ian Allan 'special', hauled from Paddington by 4–4–0 No. 3440 *City of Truro* and 2–6–0 No. 6313, outside Swindon works on 10 April 1958.

Mike Vinten

When I look back now at Swindon works, it seems unbelievable the variety and complexity of the place, where raw materials came in and wagons, coaches, locomotives and much more came out, new or repaired. These days factories may make a vehicle, but components come in from all over the world. Now even locomotives are imported from the US, and the new trains for Heathrow express are imported from Spain. How the mighty have fallen – or have they been tripped and pushed?

The social highlights were the leaving parties, when lads had finished their 'time inside' and were either going back to their home depots, which could be anywhere on the Western region, into the services to do National Service, or some into the Merchant Navy in preference to National Service. These parties usually took over one of the down town pubs on the apprentice's last Thursday evening, and as there was usually a large Welsh contingent a few pints and the 'choir' in them rose to the surface with all the rousing rugby, pop and Welsh songs that they could muster. There never seemed to be any trouble afterwards – but, of course, the pubs closed at 10.30pm or 11.00pm in those days.

I also remember one of my journeys back to Swindon on a Sunday evening being disrupted by the derailment of a South Wales – Paddington excursion train near Didcot. But, in those days, trains managed to get through (there was no bus substitution at the slightest hint of trouble, as at present), yet it was still a sad sight passing the derailed 70026 *Polar Star* and its coaches down the bank. At the same time it also made me realise what a great organisation British Railways was, able to cope with any emergency and having the equipment, expertise and personnel on hand to keep things moving.

When my apprenticeship was fast coming to a close, I applied for a transfer to Newton Abbot, where the steam loco works was being rebuilt to service diesel hydraulic locos; these were being built at Swindon and at the Glasgow works of the North British Loco Co. in readiness to oust steam from the West of England by the end of 1964. The transfer, though, was not quite as easy as that! First I had to have an interview with the divisional motive power superintendent! His headquarters were in the railway station frontage building at Newton Abbot. The building is still there, but that is about all, for Newton Abbot has slipped from being a Great Western Railway town and junction to not much more than a passing loop. There are now not even any freight facilities there. Yet a spark is ready to be rekindled if English, Welsh & Scottish Railway, the privatised freight company, have their way and promote the Heathfield line.

The interview over, I was offered a job at Laira as a locomotive fitter. The transformation of Newton Abbot's old steam locomotive works into a diesel hydraulic depot was still far from complete, and there would be no vacancies there for about a year. Laira, on the other hand, was already being supplied with these diesel hydraulic locos in ever-increasing numbers and needed extra staff immediately.

So, in October 1961, I found steam banished to the old Great Western round house at Laira and the diesels allocated to the straight shed. This area was choc-a-block with diesels, especially on night turn, when many were on depot for servicing.

I soon settled into a three-shift system, which included weekends. At Swindon I'd worked a forty-hour week, Monday to Friday, but this was the real world: locos had to be ready to work trains.

The loco accommodation was bad enough, but the staff quarters were worse! The old auto-trailer used as mess and changing rooms had seen better days, but its hot, oily, smoke-smelling ambience was much appreciated by me after a cold trip to work from Paignton on my 250 BSA motorbike on those bitterly cold early mornings of the 1960s.

Whereas the Swindon staff had been railway employees for years, father to son, Laira had a mix of experienced railway steam fitters with a large influx of men with diesel experience from the dockyard and the navy. I expect there were rifts, but on the whole everyone mucked in together very well, in quite difficult circumstances and on mostly untried equipment, under the watchful eye of the depot engineer, Len Olver.

The area allocated for the new shed was then a building site, but, as soon as track had been laid in the westernmost part, the diesel multiple units began to arrive and it was pressed into use whilst the builders worked around us. All we had were pits with rails on top, and a roof. All the walls and fittings had still to be built and fitted.

About a year later the call came to transfer to Newton Abbot as the conversion there was almost complete and staff adjustments were being made. Consequently, I could now look forward to having an easier journey to work, but looking back over my stint at Laira it is the journeys that stick in my mind most. Usually I used my bike, but the equipment we had in the 'sixties was antiquated compared with today's motorbike gear, and I froze. Snow and frost were a nightmare: the roads and the gritting were not like they are now! In complete contrast, summer mornings and evenings were bliss, and, of course, there was very little traffic before the Marples/Beeching carve up.

The trains were fine, but not for shift working or for getting from North Road (as Plymouth main station was called then) back to Laira. Sometimes a light engine running back to Laira, or even to Friary depot, was the easiest, but it was often a bus, which nearly doubled the journey time. Some of my journeys entailed getting a lift on a freight or milk train. (These days we would pay for the privilege of a footplate trip home on a steam-hauled freight from Tavistock Junction yard, if it were possible!) A hard working 'Hall' blasting up Hemerdon bank at the head of a heavy 'goods' being banked by a 'Prairie' tank or D63XX, especially on a rainy/squally night, was really something to experience. Of course, the following week I could be gliding round the curves in the cab of a brand new 'Warship', hauling the St Erth to Wood Lane milk tanks. All this has now passed into history.

Newton Abbot 83A was to be my work place for the next ten or so years – a happy depot under the control of Ron Cole, on transfer from Laira. I was back on steam for a while as I was regarded as the 'new boy'. Those days, however, soon came to an end as steam finished in 1964, at about the same time as I married a lass from

A scene at Newton Abbot on 11 November 1971 as WR 'Warship' class diesel-hydraulic No. D826 *Jupiter* leads D6318, D6323, D6322 and D815 (all destined for scrap) towards East signal box.

Mike Vinten

Lancashire. Our honeymoon in the south of France at Cassis was great, especially as they still had large oil-burning steam locos called 141R 2–8–2s working all along the coast from Marseilles to Nice. Sylvia, my wife, still has to put up with railway visits on holidays, and if there is any steam that is a bonus!

The years at Newton passed smoothly, the youngish staff becoming experienced with the new locos, getting married, having children, buying houses, or making other commitments, until suddenly the British Rail Board decided to standardise on diesel-electric traction. The motorways and Beeching, between them, had devastated the freight traffic, and many closed lines meant a surplus of locomotives and servicing facilities, so savings had to be made. Furthermore, although Newton Abbot did a better job more economically than any other Western Region depot – figures proved it – and Bill Thomas did a good job as shop representative, the Board's mind was made up and the depot closed. Bill must have enjoyed his political christening, for he caught the bug and became a town councillor.

With the closure, staff were offered posts at various hard-to-fill locations – Old Oak Common (West London), Newport, and the Severn Tunnel. Many took up the offer, but found commuting too much of a struggle and gave up, some thrived and soon became supervisors and managers, while others, including myself, decided to stay put and had a stay of execution for a year, working on plant and track maintenance machinery.

At the same time I received an offer of an eventual post in Bristol, but this I subsequently declined and, instead, managed to stay work-free for three months, despite job offers cropping up much too often! I wanted to work on the house, put in central heating and enjoy life. Eventually I gave in and took a job with a local engineering firm, but the boredom/monotony of the first day drove me to ask for my 'cards' on the second! However, the boss suggested that I stayed for a few weeks to strip down and move some machinery, which was more in my line. On completing this job, I then started working for a local central heating firm installing central heating systems. This was much more interesting, especially seeing the different environments in which people live – from mansions to filthy hovels: I could not believe it!

By that spring (1973) the private Dart Valley Railway Company had taken over the Paignton-Kingswear line and I had the opportunity to become the resident fitter there, even though the main workshop and maintenance staff were based at Buckfastleigh.

As a result, my work now varied from repairing vandalised station buildings, such as those at Goodrington Halt, to spending all day and half the night keeping the locos running; these included the little (former GWR) tank engines used on the school trains which were all part of an all-the-year-round public service provided in the very early days of the DVR. However, the great draw of that first year was the recently returned *Flying Scotsman* from America. It put the railway on the map, but it certainly caused a few headaches, even though it was looked after like a baby by its own fitter. The worst trouble to befall it that summer was badly worn driving wheel tyres: the combination of continually running up and down the tightly curved branch line without being turned, combined with suspected higher than the permitted light railway speed limit of 25mph, caused excessive flange wear. This meant my ex-Newton Abbot foreman, Reg Smale, and I spending three days with hand grinders in a siding near Kingswear, dressing the wheels to bring them back within gauge. A wonderful place to work on summer days!

Another near-calamitous day was when, following a boiler wash

The *Flying Scotsman* passing Goodrington yard during a tour of duty with the Dart Valley Railway Company on the Paignton to Kingswear line.

Rev. D. Hardy

out, a mud hole door joint blew out and sent a roaring jet of boiling water and steam across the 'down' main line platform at Paignton. Amazingly no-one was injured, as usually there was a knot of people looking through the railings at the happenings in the Dart Valley yard.

I enjoyed my experiences with the DVR but, one day, when the boss at Laira told me that the diesel hydraulics (or what was left of them) were being concentrated at his depot and that there was now a job for a number of the ex-Newton Abbot staff, I decided on big brother again. Consequently, for the second time, I started at Laira, only on this occasion in the new shed (now twelve years old or more!).

The D1000 class, or 'Westerns', as they were called – all their names were prefixed by 'Western' – were destined to end their days on freight and passenger trains to and from the Westcountry. In fact, their days were already numbered, partly because of BR's preference for diesel-electric traction, and partly because the new generation of coaches were electrically heated or air-conditioned whereas the 'Westerns' had only steam heating. So, by the mid-'seventies, the 50 class had ousted our good-looking 'Westerns' and taken over the main line trains, often working in pairs until Laira modified them so as to improve their reliability. Engine-wise, they were going back in time – a great carthorse of a unit compared with the racehorse style of the 'Westerns'. Still, by the 'eighties, the 50s were on a downward spiral, being ousted from main line trains, due to the advent of the high speed trains (HSTs), and relegated to reliefs and the Waterloo route from Exeter.

In much the same way the diesel multiple units gave way to the 'Skippers', 'Sprinters' and 'Express' units. However, the 'Skippers' did not last long in the Westcountry because of their long, fixed wheel-base, which made the wheels screech on the rails and caused excessive tyre and rail wear on the branch lines: the Victorians had realised that bogies were required on passenger vehicles over 100 years ago! As a result, the 'Skippers', which had another innovation in the form of cable-operated brakes, were soon exiled to the north of England, where they had yet a worse design of unit, which has at last been put to rest.

The next big change was sectorisation, which began in the late 'eighties as a prelude to privatisation. Each type of traffic was accounted for separately, the different sectors painting their stock in different liveries so as to give themselves an identity. At Laira, we began painting the class 50 locos for the Waterloo service in Network South East red, white and blue livery. However, the corporate blue livery of 'good old BR' was in decline, and this was something that continued until the eventual privatisation programme had been completed

I was caught up in all of this, and in the early 'nineties became the area maintenance supervisor for the Exeter area, working for RFD (Railfreight Distribution), which had been allotted Exeter loco depot and the freight yards of Taunton, Exeter and Plymouth. The area also included Bridgwater, Meldon Quarry and Yeovil, and the nucleus of staff were fitters at Exeter St David's depot, servicing locos and diesel multiple units, and attending any calls to breakdowns in the area. These members of staff were, in turn, supported by RSTs (Rolling Stock Technicians), who undertook all train examining (passenger and freight) and any running maintenance that could be done without stopping a particular vehicle. They were scattered around the area and were in touch with the 'A' team (as we called them), who would attend any larger jobs requiring attention in the out-of-the-way locations.

Not long after arriving at Exeter I found myself in the consultation procedures to amalgamate the RST and shunters in all the freight yards, for BR had decided that examiners were also to be earmarked for redundancy as the Exeter-Waterloo loco-hauled trains were to be replaced with diesel units of the 159 class. Again normal procedures were followed: all the examiners were approaching retirement age and accepted severance without too much acrimony.

I am still the area maintenance supervisor for the Exeter area, only now employed by Wales & West Passenger Trains Ltd. Like the other TOCs (Train Operating Companies), this company does not own its own trains but hires them from ROSCO – three companies set up at privatisation to take over the ownership of all the rolling stock. Similarly, it does not own any track: that has to be hired from Railtrack! Nevertheless, if Wales & West, or any other TOC, does not run, runs late or holds up other TOC trains, it is penalised. If Railtrack, on the other hand, cannot supply the track as stated, a fine is imposed.

I have enjoyed my life working on the railway and, hopefully, still have a few more years to go. I also hope that my wife and I will be able to continue to visit some of the more outlandish places that the 'iron road' serves.

❋❋❋❋❋

3. (a) ENGINE DRIVER
(b) LORRY DRIVER

(a) Mr Colin Pulleyblank continued a family tradition, begun by his grandfather, when he joined the Great Western Railway in 1938:–

The arrival of the railway was the basis for the growth of Newton Abbot, in Devon, where my family lived. Various jobs were suddenly created, and as the number of employees grew, from about 1850 onwards, so extra housing was needed to accommodate the railway workers and their families. The result was that whole new areas were developed, one of the first being from East Street to Decoy. Later, the Broadlands and Buckland Estates were also created; then Laurie Estate, which was purpose-built for railway employees only.

Throughout this period of growth many railwaymen started contributing to town life – as mayors, chairmen of councils, justices of the peace and so on, or became involved in other public services. The railwaymen also formed a branch of the old Social & Educational Society (later to become the Staff Association) and built Forde Hall as a social centre to cater for various interests of the 'railway family'.

My first personal involvement with the railway, albeit indirectly, was when I was twelve years old and acted as a patient for the local railway ambulance team, for which my father was leader. The superintendent at the railway remembered this when I left school and asked my father, who worked as a carriage and wagon examiner, if I wanted work. So, at the age of fourteen, during the depression of the 'thirties, I was fortunate enough to be offered a job as a rivet boy in the engine repair factory of the GWR at Newton Abbot.

Many employees came from families that had long connections with the GWR, among them those who had survived the First World War and knew my father. They looked after me as 'Polly's boy'.

Over the years the engines, carriages and wagons were improved in design and expertise. I witnessed the introduction of electric welding to repair engine main frames (1" steel plate fractures); this saved time and expense, and was stronger than a plate fixed to the main frame by 300 rivets. I also learned about the construction of railway engines in the factory and this helped fulfil my future ambition to be an engine driver.

My eighteen months as a rivet boy quickly passed and I transferred to the Newton Abbot locomotive running shed to become an engine cleaner. However, by then the Second World War had started, and cleaners were required to upgrade, temporarily, to engine fireman in order to cope with the extra war trains. Consequently, I did not clean many locomotives and, instead, I learned the art of firing a steam engine to keep a head of steam to the requirements and satisfaction of the driver – at the fireman's rate of pay, which was useful.

In May 1941 I was made a fireman and sent to Oxford at the age of 17 years 3 months. It was strange being away from home for the first time and fending for myself, but I was lucky really as other fellows, who were not in reserved occupations, were called up and endured the horror of fighting, many being injured or killed.

I was well trained on the railway at Newton Abbot, and the Oxford drivers recognised this and I was readily accepted. The terrain around Oxford was mostly flat, very different from our hilly Devon. After leaving work at 3am, I used to dread walking cautiously along the canal footpath near the water in the black-out in a dense fog. I thought of the possible consequences! However, I enjoyed my six months at Oxford and then returned to Newton Abbot in October 1941.

I resumed my duties there with old mates and friends that I had grown up with. Very often I was firing for a driver who was the father of a schoolmate, so the family atmosphere continued. During the war we were expected to work long hours on all types of trains such as during the evacuation from Dunkirk – difficult circumstances for all grades of railwaymen. Newton Abbot depot was always involved in work from the top long-distance passenger trains down to the bottom grade of stopping goods trains. West of Newton Abbot the terrain becomes hilly (banks in the railway terms) requiring extra engine power: this was primarily the reason for the importance of Newton Abbot as a railway location.

There were several attacks by German bombers and in one

particularly vicious raid on Newton Abbot 14 people were killed, while a further 61 were injured, 15 seriously. Fifteen engines, 56 carriages and 22 wagons were also damaged, along with parts of the station, track and workshops. My father's ambulance experience proved invaluable in helping some of the seriously injured.

When the Second World War ended life gradually returned to normal. The railway company made great efforts to revert to good timekeeping after the wartime disruptions, and there was a programme of either building new engines, carriages and wagons or refurbishing existing ones. We never lost our pride in the work and the spirit was even greater with new conditions. A better service was enjoyed by the general public, who had suffered much during the war.

Work as a fireman on steam engines was hard. I remember getting on the footplate at Newton Abbot Station to work the 1am train to Paddington, via Bristol, and looking at the tender of coal. It was full (6 tons): when it was nearly empty I knew that we were close to Paddington. Of course, there were other turns that were not so strenuous, such as trips on the Newton Abbot to Moretonhampstead line by auto train (one coach and engine as a 'push-pull'). Here, I remember working the final train of the day. After we had drawn level with the last bus from Newton Abbot (at Kelly Cross, beyond Lustleigh), there followed an exchange of whistles and bus horn. Then the drivers had a friendly race to Moreton: invariably we won! I also recall that after stabling the autocoach at Moreton we were required to run light engine back to Newton Abbot and that whilst returning one evening we saw the Moretonhampstead fire engine racing towards a burning railway embankment near Lustleigh. I then said to my driver: "I wonder who did that!"

Turns involving Paddington and Shrewsbury meant lodging away and returning home the next day. In the earlier days we had to carry our own food in what we called 'gruboxes', and this had to last until we returned home. Washing facilities were very primitive in the depots, just a concrete trough; hot water came from a stationary engine boiler – very hot, or non-existent! In some of the 'double home' lodgings bedrooms were crammed with as many beds as the landlady could manage: not very desirable! In later years hostels were available in some depots that made life easier: a nice single room and a good canteen.

In 1948 the GWR ceased to operate and British Rail (Western Region) took over, but the effect of the changeover was gradual and life continued much as usual. The following year I married Nancy Blatchford, a railwayman's daughter, and later our children, Robert and Anne, arrived. They played and went to school with children of our own school friends – three generations involved – so the family atmosphere continued.

The 'fifties saw the invasion of the Devon and Cornwall coastal resorts by visitors from all over the country, which gave us a lot of extra work in the summer. On Saturday mornings each June, July and August the Torquay 'up' platform would fill and empty every ten minutes from 8am till lunchtime. The railway police used to marshal passengers from queues just outside the station to the platform for their return trains.

My application for a driver's job in Exeter was successful in August 1959. It was only twenty miles from Newton Abbot, but that made a great deal of difference to our family life because I did not own a car and had to rely on trains for transport to and from work. The awkward train times that footplate staff were required

Exeter St David's, where WR 'Warship' class diesel-hydraulic No. 819 *Goliath* is seen passing Exeter Middle signal box with a Plymouth to Liverpool train on 7 September 1963. On the banker spur in the centre of the photograph, and standing by for duty, are two 'W' class 2–6–4Ts, Nos. 31924 & 31914, and 0–6–0PT No. 4692.

Mike Vinten

to work, and the availability of suitable trains, did not match: I spent hours waiting to go to and from work. Family life became slightly strained as I was away from home so much.

I had anticipated that my stay in Exeter would be a short one and that my problems would soon be over. Unfortunately, the management of British Rail lacked the compassion of the old superintendent of the GWR and that, combined with the government interference in the form of Dr Beeching, meant that I did not return to Newton Abbot at all. In the meantime, diesels replaced steam trains, and eventually the high-speed locomotives were used on nearly all express trains.

My stay at Exeter was 30 years until I retired. A car had eventually improved my travel arrangements but, even so, I still lost many hours because of the commuting. However, the pay for the job did at least provide us with a reasonable lifestyle.

During the last eight years of my job in the top link (group of trains) I became the district committeeman of the old Great Western Railway Enginemen and Firemens' Mutual Assurance Sick and Superannuation Society, work which I enjoyed. In 1865 the generous directors of the GWR had encouraged the formation of the pension fund, to the envy of all the other railway companies' employees, and I now had to arrange the pensions for the newly retired footplate staff, also the widows' allowances and assist any widow in difficulty. In its heyday our society had paid a widow's pension of 12/6d to add to the State widow's pension of 10/– each week. Sadly, though, the Society was dissolved after 130 years' service to members, when British Rail started their own pension scheme and starved it of new members.

I enjoyed my 50 years and 18 weeks as a railwayman and was proud to be one of the old 'God's Wonderful Railway' employees.

✳✳✳✳✳

(b) Mr Reginald G. Salter was born in Willand (near Cullompton) in 1906 and worked on the railway for over 47 years, several of these as a lorry driver:–

My father was a ganger on the Great Western Railway, in charge of six lengthmen at Cullompton, but retired in 1928. Two of my brothers were also employed on the GWR, one as a parcels porter at Wellington and Taunton; the other as a signalman at Thorverton, on the Exe Valley line, but he later emigrated to Canada.

We lived at Willand, where all the family was born. While he was working, Dad had to leave at 6.30am and did not get home again until about 6.30pm. He worked very hard as in those days everything was done by hand. Sometimes the gang had to work on Sundays, relaying the track with another gang from Taunton or Exeter depots. The work had to be finished in a day and sometimes it took twelve hours.

They used wooden sleepers on the track in those days and the rails were kept in place by wooden keys, which would fall out in hot weather; so Dad had to walk his length of rail on Sundays with his hammer and knock them back into place. In the summer the grass on the banks had to be cut by a gang with scythes, and the farmers had the hay.

I was eight years old when the First World War began. We boys then used to go to Tiverton Junction Station on Sundays in order to watch the troop trains and the Red Cross trains taking the wounded from France, once they had docked at Plymouth; sadly, my oldest brother was one of the many killed on the Somme. Whilst there, we also saw lots of other trains, with their green engines and chocolate coaches, and I recall how we could almost set our watches by the *Torbay Express* and *Cornish Riviera Limited* as they went past.

At that time Tiverton Junction was a busy station: it had a parcels office and porters who used to transfer the parcels between the branch line trains from Exeter (via the Exe Valley line) and those which travelled to Hemyock and back on the Culm Valley line, and there was also a cleaner who attended to the 'local' engine and the coal every day. The trains that ran on the Culm Valley line, incidentally, were usually 'mixed' (one passenger coach, plus goods wagons), and we called the small engine 'Puffing Billy' because the line was quite steep out from the junction and it did not always make it at the first attempt!

Tiverton Junction, as 4–6–0 No. 6003 *King George IV* thunders through on the *Cornish Riviera Limited*, 10.30am Paddington to Penzance, on 5 August 1957.

Peter W. Gray

There was also a busy factory at Tiverton Junction called the Duchess of Devonshire, producing butter, cream, cheese, etc., which went to various parts of the country. In those days, of course, nearly every town and village had a station or halt, and connections could be made to almost anywhere.

After the war there was a lot of unemployment; men coming back from active service or the mines, etc., so there were few vacancies available on the railways. I left school aged fourteen and went straight into a job at a big house called Townlands, where they wanted a lad to work in the gardens. Dad had put my name down for any vacancy that might occur on the railway, but it was not until I was aged nearly eighteen that there was a position on the Chard branch, at Hatch Beauchamp. I had to go to Exeter to see an inspector called Mapledoram and pass a medical examination before I was accepted.

I was sent to Hatch on Boxing Day, 1923. When I arrived the stationmaster said: "You are the new boy; you will need lodgings, so when the signalman goes to the village he will fix you up. In the meantime, I will give you a broom and you can sweep the platform." In those days stationmasters were very strict: we had to knock on the door before entering, take our cap off and always wear uniform.

There were passenger and goods trains on the branch in those days. The goods trains had station trucks, where the goods were unloaded on to the platform; then I had to take them to the goods shed by trolley. We had a goods yard, where trucks of coal, cattle food and other goods were shunted. I attended to the lamps in the signals, cleaned the windows, etc., but I was not at Hatch for long before being sent to Bishop's Lydeard (on the Minehead branch),

BR standard class 3 2–6–2T No. 82030 running non-stop through Bishop's Lydeard with the last of three Saturday through trains from Minehead to Paddington at 3.30pm on 20 July 1963. Just visible in the distance is a diesel multiple-unit set forming the 3.25pm from Taunton to Minehead local service, and also the signalman standing outside his box on the 'up' platform waiting to collect the single line token from the fireman.

Peter W. Gray

which was a busier station. We had a station yard where a lot more work was done and we also had a coal depot. There were two signalmen and the stationmaster, and there were more trains. I enjoyed my stay at Bishop's Lydeard and it was there that I met my wife, who worked in the local post office. After two years I was sent to Ilminster, back on the Chard branch again. I had to work in the goods department – a very busy place. There were two horses which delivered the goods to the town.

We had a big yard where the goods trains, which ran every day, used to shunt the wagons, leave the full ones and take the empties, and there was a signal box open twenty-four hours a day. A post office train ran from Taunton to Chard during the night, so we had a signal porter and two signalmen, clerks in the goods department, a parcel porter, stationmaster and booking clerk. There was a milk factory which sent syphons of milk away every day, including Sundays.

In 1929 a change took place: the horses were sent back to Bristol and a lorry came to take their place. The older horse driver retired; the younger one learned to drive. This was happening all over England, as the railway lost traffic to the roads. I was given the chance to learn to drive and an offer to go to South Molton in order to open a country lorry service. I used to deliver the goods to the town first, then go out to farms in the afternoons. Some places had never seen a lorry before and some lanes were so narrow that a horse and cart had to be brought out to collect the goods.

As I had an increase in pay from £2.0.0d to £2.2.6d (£2.13p) my fiancée and I felt that we could afford to marry, which we did on 30 July 1930, after courting for five years; we have now been married 68 years. We paid 7/6d rent for a small house.

I was at South Molton for two years and then offered a parcel driver's post at Tiverton. Tiverton was a busy station and I

A view of Tiverton Station on 4 August 1962 as 0–4–2T No. 1462 on the 7.50am Exeter to Dulverton local service connects with sister engine No. 1466 on the Tiverton to Tiverton Junction auto train.
Mike Vinten

With holiday traffic on the branch at its peak over the August Bank Holiday period of 1938, GWR 'Bulldog' class 4–4–0 tender engine No. 3443 *Chaffinch* is turned on the turntable at Minehead engine shed in readiness for working a return excursion train to Taunton. Meanwhile, GWR '45XX' class 2–6–2T No. 5542 waits on the spare road outside the engine shed before working a normal service train later in the day.

Simon P. Bowditch

53

delivered thousands of parcels there during the 18 years of my stay. There were five lorries in the goods department, which made deliveries over a large area. There was also a large brewery, Starkey Knight, and the John Heathcoat factory, both of which sent goods by train all over the country. The boys from Blundell's School also kept me busy when they went home after every term and then returned to school after the holiday. We had hundreds of trunks, tuck boxes and bicycles; the trunks and tuck boxes were sent for 1/– each (luggage in advance) and they had to be delivered at five different houses. They all came by train in those days.

I had not been well for some time and the doctor advised me to get a lighter job, so when the opportunity arose with a vacancy at Taunton, in 1950, for a ticket collector, I accepted. I then had to learn all about tickets, and my job was to examine those on the branch line trains on the Minehead, Chard and Barnstaple services, and also to relieve at the barriers. We were busy in those days; so many used the trains before cars had taken over. We had a cleaning staff which kept the coaches and windows clean.

It was sad when the Chard and Barnstaple lines closed. I was promoted and travelled on the main lines; on the *Mayflower* to London for two weeks and then to Newton Abbot, Bristol and Bath on the third.

When we had steam trains we left Paddington on Friday evenings at 5.30pm, with thirteen coaches, two engines and over 1,000 passengers. It took me the whole of the journey to Taunton to examine the tickets and, if necessary, to charge excess on some fares. Then we took all the people back again on Sunday evenings. The fares from Taunton to Paddington in those days were 29s.10d (First Class) and 17s.11d (Third Class), and the journey took nearly three hours.

Then the change came from steam to diesel and we had a problem when some drivers did not know what to do when something failed. Often we had to wait for another engine – and the passengers were not too pleased!

I was a passenger guard for my last three years on the railway: the guards did the work of the ticket examiners on the trains. I was on the Minehead branch as guard the last week before it closed, which was also the week before I retired in February 1971, after 47 years on the railway.

❋❋❋❋❋

4. SHUNTER

Mr Fred Kearley joined the railway in February 1948, about two months after nationalisation:-

I began work as a messenger boy and later became a shunter at Old Oak Common, the large yard in the Acton area of London. However, by 1956 I had a wife and two children and could not find suitable housing in London, so was offered accommodation at Swindon. It was bitterly cold there and on the first morning that I began work at the yard the foreman greeted me by saying: "Tis main tarblish this morning, sno you". I thought, "My God, I've gone abroad", but I soon became accustomed to the Wiltshire dialect.

Swindon was one of the great railway workshops of the world and employed between 22,000 and 23,000 people. Every area had its own shunting pilot (the engine that does the shunting) and shunters. Next to the station was a small yard that dealt with the nearby workshops' traffic. The shunter in charge had a most unusual musical talent. He could play various tunes on his whistle 'Acme Thunder Mark I'. 'Come to the Cookhouse Door' surprised me, but when I heard him play that old tune 'Back to Sorrento' I was stunned.

The factory closed down for the summer holiday during the first two weeks of July. For some reason these were called 'Trip weeks'. The Wednesday in the first week was known at 'Trip Wednesday' and many shops in town closed all day, but I recall this happening only once or twice. The influx of people like myself from other areas, many of whom did not work on the railway, soon put an end to that tradition. Oddly enough, it nearly always rained in Swindon during Trip.

The run-up to Trip was marked by a heavy increase in the number of vehicles leaving the shops and coming into service. Most of these were vehicles that had been repaired, and we had the job of disposing of them. We would attach them to any train going in the right direction. I remember one train, that normally went with five on, going out with twelve. I wanted to put another four on it, but the inspector put his foot down.

The workers used to book their holidays at work, and if there were a sufficient number of them a special train was laid on to any destination. It was odd to see trains going to places like Blackpool, Margate and Yarmouth leaving Swindon Station. These were all specials, and although they numbered dozens they never interrupted the normal service. It was a clever piece of railway organisation, and I was very impressed. When I commented on this I was told: "This is nothing to what it was in the old days." But what is?

An overall view of Swindon works, c1960.

Mike Vinten

Working outdoors meant that we were very much at the mercy of the weather. I suppose the most worrying thing was fog, especially after dark. Fortunately, they were never as bad as the London smogs. But, even so, no-one liked them, and trying to signal with those old oil lamps, or using our whistle – all of which sounded the same – tended to make us very, very careful.

Rain wasn't much fun, either. In the early days we were issued with a rubberised twill mac and leggings, with a Sou'wester (or, as one wag insisted on calling it, a South Western). This clothing was fine whilst it was new, but, with wear and oil getting on it, it leaked like a sieve. Consequently, we soon became soaked to the skin and this, in turn, made us feel very cold.

When I think of wind, I remember the biting east wind that blew across the sidings. I am sure that it came straight from Siberia but, whatever, it certainly cut through any amount of clothing. One day I had a tear freeze in my eye and saw a man's lips split and chap under the lash of that wind. I am sure it blows in Hell!

I was on night duty when one of the blizzards of 1963 hit us. The chap with whom I was working had a beard, and as he clawed the snow out of it he said: "This is not a blizzard, you know". When I asked why, he said: "Because you can't hear the wind howling". I am sure the snow was leaving the cloud base twenty miles away before it hit the ground. It felt like a wet towel slapping your face and it stung like mad, yet he didn't believe it was a blizzard. I didn't know whether to laugh, cry, or kick him on the shin. In the end I said: "Let's go and have a cup of tea". A much better idea.

The snow remained for weeks; then a steady downpour of rain hastened the thaw. I remember this well because on one occasion at around that time, whilst in wet-weather gear, I dropped down off the platform on to the line to couple some vehicles when suddenly a cascade of water came off the station verandah roof and covered me. As it splashed on my face I realised it was was perfumed and quite warm: it transpired that one of the girls from the refreshment rooms (who lodged above the station) had had a bath and an obstruction in the pipe leading to the gutter had caused the water to drown me!

I eventually left Swindon in 1975 after having spent around nineteen years there, all but the first eighteen months or so employed as a Class 1 shunter, following promotion. During that time about thirty married men had jobs as Class I shunters. One man was told by his doctor that if he did not leave the work his wife would have a mental breakdown: he resigned at once. The wives of two other men did end up in mental hospitals for a short time, and six marriages (including mine) ended in divorce. It showed, I think, the stupidity of putting your job before your family.

❋❋❋❋❋

5. EXAMINER

Mr Ken Mapp was just fourteen years old in October 1945 when he began working for the Southern Railway as an oiler and greaser in the carriage and wagon department, based at Exmouth Junction:–

When I started on the railway, at Exmouth Junction, my pay was just 32s. 6d. (£1.62p) per week and I had to do shift work (6am to 2pm one week, 10pm to 6am the next and then 2pm to 10pm during the third week), attending the many freight trains arriving at the depot. At that time most of the wagons had journals and bearings which were lubricated by grease, and part of my job was

[Not to Scale]

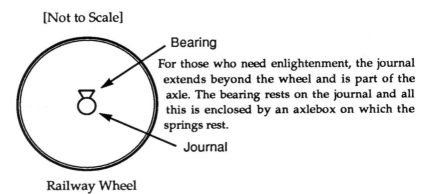

Bearing

For those who need enlightenment, the journal extends beyond the wheel and is part of the axle. The bearing rests on the journal and all this is enclosed by an axlebox on which the springs rest.

Journal

Railway Wheel

to top up their grease boxes above each of the axleboxes, for as the journals became warm so the grease melted. This, in turn, meant having to carry heavy buckets of grease and, sometimes, returning to the grease house for a further supply. A freight train leaving Salisbury, for example, would have grease boxes topped up at Yeovil Junction, Axminster and then at Exmouth Junction.

I worked with an examiner all of the time. His job was to examine each train and, if he found a defective vehicle, to put red 'not to go' cards on the vehicle concerned, whereupon the shunters had to remove it from the train. He also tapped all of the wheels to ensure there were no slack or cracked tyres. Most of the trains in those days were unfitted, meaning that they did not have a vacuum-brake system throughout. Consequently, there was a guard's brakevan at the rear, and it was the job of the guard to apply the handbrake when the train was going down a gradient. Sometimes, if the train had a full load, the wheels and brake blocks became almost red hot, and there were occasions when my examiner and I would have to fit new blocks to the brakevan in between trains. These brake blocks weighed about 1cwt each and, as a young lad, I had to sit on the railway line and get one on my knee so that it was high enough for me to fit. At that time there were also some wagons that were fitted with oil axleboxes, mainly those with a vacuum-brake system, which was controlled by the driver of the train. Some trains had all the wagons fitted with vacuum brakes; one of these was the 9.10pm from Nine Elms, in London, to Plymouth, detaching vehicles at Salisbury and Exeter. Most of the vehicles contained perishable goods, and this train, known as the 'Tavy', was due in Exeter at about 2.30am.

It was yet another part of our job to oil these vehicles, which was done every two months. Every six months they also had to have a pad examination, as after a while pads which soaked up the oil to lubricate journals and bearings would become glazed, causing a hot box. This meant that bearings which were of brass and white metal melted with the heat and a new pair of wheels would have to be fitted, as the journal became scored. When a hot box did occur, it caused a high-pitched screaming sound that could be heard from about a quarter of a mile away.

After working for three weeks at Exmouth Junction we moved to Exeter Central, where most of the work was on passenger trains. Here, we worked four turns of duty – 6am to 2pm; 10pm to 6am; 2pm to 10pm and 10am to 6pm – and it was our job to feel all the axleboxes on the platform side of the passenger trains so as to ensure that they were not running hot. We also carried a large can of oil so that if we found an axlebox overheating we could put oil in the axlebox and lubricating pads. When feeling the axleboxes, if a train had ten vehicles, it meant that we had to bend down forty times!

On the 6am to 2pm shift we went to outstations in order to carry out repairs and patch up any wagons put off with hot axleboxes, so that we could get them to Exmouth Junction wagon shops for new wheels to be fitted. On the 10am to 6pm shift we carried out oiling and pad examination on passenger coaches, and helped with repairs.

All trains at that time were hauled by steam locomotives, and the passenger coaches were heated by steam. Sometimes the rubber steam pipes between the coaches burst and we had to fit new ones.

On the outstation turn we covered, to the east, as far as Sidmouth, which had a branch line coming off the Waterloo route. This was at Sidmouth Junction, now called Feniton, but the Sidmouth branch was later closed by Dr Beeching. At that time, though, passenger coaches were detached from Waterloo trains at Sidmouth Junction for passengers going to Sidmouth. These coaches were then returned to Sidmouth Junction on the following day and attached to an Exeter to Waterloo train.

The outstation turn also meant covering as far as Eggesford, on the Barnstaple/Ilfracombe line, and the stations on the main line to Plymouth and North Cornwall; this, too, was later closed by Dr Beeching, but is still used by freight trains as far as Meldon Quarry for the collection of ballast for use on railway lines.

In 1949, a year after the former Southern Railway had become the Southern Region of British Railways due to nationalisation, I applied successfully for a vacancy as a senior oiler at Templecombe, in Somerset. The work here was similar to that at Exmouth Junction, involving mainly freight trains, and there were two marshalling yards; the upper was on the Exeter to Waterloo line and the other, called the Midland yard, belonged to the Midland Region of BR, originally the Somerset and Dorset line. Passengers wishing to get to Bournemouth had to change at Templecombe, but this was yet another line that was destined to fall under the Beeching axe.

I was called up for National Service in the RAF in August 1949, so was away from the railway for two years. During that time I was advised by the Southern Region that I had been appointed as a repairer at Bricklayers Arms, in London, on 18 October 1949: this position I declined. Similarly, I did not accept an appointment as examiner at Clapham Junction on 27 March 1950.

After my two years service in the RAF, I returned to Exeter Central as a carriage serviceman. Most of this work involved the repair and maintenance of coaching stock, and, now and again, working on derailments, re-railing vehicles.

When a vacancy for an examiner occurred at Exeter in 1952, I applied, but to become an examiner meant passing a test on rules

'Bridge 118'. Rebuilt 'Westcountry' class Pacific No. 34046 *Braunton* crosses the West of England main line at Cole, near Bruton, Somerset with the 10.35am (Saturdays only) service from Bournemouth West to Manchester, which took the S. & D.J.R. route over the Mendip Hills. Passing under the bridge in this scene from the summer of 1960 is former GWR '2884' class 2–8–0 No. 3850 as it attacks the 1 in 98 gradient of Brewham Bank with a Banbury-bound freight train.

Simon P. Bowditch

and regulations and studying a book called 'An Examiner's Guide Book'. On the Southern Region we also had to spend two weeks at Grovener Road sidings in London. These were attached to Victoria Station, all the lines being attached to the third rail electrified line, which carried 750 volts. Not being used to this live line made me step very high!

While I was at Grovener Road I saw the *Golden Arrow* arrive from Paris each morning. Railwaymen called it the 'blue train' because it was composed of French sleeping cars which were all painted blue. I then went to London Bridge Station and was passed out as an examiner on 5 May 1952, subsequently taking up duty in the examiners' link at Exeter Central and Exmouth Junction.

In the early 'sixties the Southern Region decided to expand a yard at Yeoford, a station just beyond Crediton and near to where the lines to North Devon and Plymouth diverged. Trains for North Cornwall and North Devon were marshalled here, and the turns of duty were 12.01am to 10am and 4pm to 1am. The yard, which had only six roads, but was very long, boasted no electric lighting, only tilley lamps, and seemed to be in the middle of nowhere!

Our accommodation was a Great Western box wagon, which had been fitted out with a coal fire, range, table, chair and wash basin, and there was a pair of steps to get into it: water had to be fetched from a shunter's cabin.

At that time we were still using a carbide lamp for examining trains. This consisted of carbide of calcium in a chamber in the bottom and a water tank in the top: the water dripped on to the carbide, so giving off a gas which was then ignited. The result was a very bright light which would illuminate a wide area, showing the whole of a wagon.

It was in 1963 that the Beeching axe fell on the railways: more branch lines were closed. One of these was the line from Axminster to Lyme Regis, so the examiners at Axminster were made redundant and Exeter took over as far as Chard Junction. At that time we maintained milk tanks at Seaton Junction and Chard Junction, but the only way to get to these places was by bus once the stations had closed.

When the Western Region took over parts of the Southern Region in 1967 all coaching stock went to Newton Abbot for maintenance. At around the same time the work of Exmouth Junction yard was transferred to Exeter Riverside, and Exmouth Junction locomotive sheds were shut down. As a result, I was

Loaded milk tanks, destined for Waterloo, leaving the yard at Seaton Junction behind ex-Southern Railway 'S15' class 4–6–0 No. 30823 on 11 June 1962.

Peter W. Gray

made redundant and offered an examiner's post at Exeter St David's Station, but by that time diesel locomotives had been introduced, and the work was that of examining passenger trains: as all of the Waterloo trains were now starting from St David's, we spent most of our time working on these.

Soon after the move to St David's it was decided that class 33 locomotives should haul the Waterloo trains. But as these locomotives could not steam-heat a train they were equipped for electric train heating (ETH) and this meant that we had to learn about it by attending a course at Newton Abbot. As time went on all trains became heated in this manner, and the braking systems were changed from vacuum brakes to air brakes, which operated on 72 $\frac{1}{2}$ lbs of air.

Shortly afterwards, it was decided that Newton Abbot should close as a locomotive and maintenance depot and that the work there should be taken over by Laira depot, at Plymouth. Because of this, many members of the staff at Newton Abbot were made redundant and our area was extended, as the Heathfield branch line was still being used for ball clay and oil traffic. This extension to the area also meant that we had to go to Goodrington on summer Saturdays in order to examine the passenger trains that terminated there.

On one of these Saturdays I was called upon to go to Goodrington in order to examine the *Orient Express*. This was because it had been on the privately-owned Paignton to Kingswear line for a short while and had to be examined by a BR examiner before it could be allowed to make its return journey to Waterloo. The job completed, and knowing that the locomotive would have to be reversed at St David's Station, I then saw the engineer who travelled with the train, told him that I had to return to Exeter and obtained his agreement for me to ride back on the *Orient Express*. This was a new experience for me as I had never travelled in a Pullman before: all the passengers were drinking champagne!

Later, our area was extended again and we were then relieving at Tavistock Junction, Plymouth and Taunton, which meant covering as far as Bridgwater and Yeovil, and also Meldon Quarry.

Eventually, Southern Region decided to have class 159 diesel units built for locomotives and coaches, and these were to be maintained at a new depot built at Salisbury. This meant that we lost all our work on the Waterloo trains. After that I was employed mainly on traction maintenance at Exeter, refuelling locomotives and diesel units, and carrying out repair work, such as renewing brake blocks. I was also on call to trains at St David's, a situation that continued until I was made redundant in 1994, after 49 years on the railway. I was then 63 years old and glad to go to bed at night knowing that there would be no more early turns or night work.

*****

6. SIGNALMAN/ INSPECTOR

Mr Bernard Price was born in 1927 in Coleham, within earshot of the Shrewsbury locomotive sheds:–

I was born into a railway family: my father was a GWR fireman and his father was a Great Western/London Midland & Scottish joint railway signalman. These joint railways covered trains through Chester to Birkenhead and from Shrewsbury to Wellington and Hereford. The GWR then took over from Wellington towards Paddington and from Hereford to Swansea, via Cardiff. At the same time the LMS had running powers over the lines from Craven Arms to Shrewsbury and the North.

My mother's father was a GWR engineering crane driver stationed at Penzance. One of his jobs, in the 'thirties, was to position the sea-defence rocks alongside Penzance Station.

When I was aged fifteen I reported to the stationmaster at Shrewsbury Station. He asked me to write out two messages about how the 8.15am Penzance to Liverpool and the 11.50am Swansea High Street to Manchester trains were running. I knew that junior porters (young boys) wrote similar messages to hand to the inspector and yard foreman, there being no such things as automatic telephones until the late 1950s to early '60s: the only phones available at that time were the 'bus line' types, covering approximately ten miles. However, each signal box station had its own call, such as 2.1, 2.2, 3.2, and on such lines everyone was able to talk. In fact, on the night turn it was common for up to six signalmen on a section of line to talk throughout the shift. Some of them worked together for twenty years or more and knew all about one another without ever having met.

Having presented my two messages to the stationmaster, I was told to improve my writing. Nevertheless, I was also told that subject to supplying three references I could start work at 2pm until 10pm at Abbey Foregate signal box on Monday, 3 April 1943,

65

as a box boy. I was delighted, and was to remain there until November 1944, working the three shifts – early, late and night.

I began by not learning how to work the signal box but how to understand the various bell codes, as each train was signalled according to the head code ie: express train – four bells; and the slowest freight trains – three bells. In addition to these bell signals there were also special bell codes to cover emergencies such as a door open on a passenger train – seven bells – and for a tail lamp out when it should be burning – nine bells.

The war was waging at that time, with German bombers regularly passing overhead en route to Liverpool and Birkenhead. Shrewsbury Station was not far from Crewe Bank box, which was destroyed, yet we suffered few air attacks. I was fascinated by the very small gas light in the signal box, which had a black tin mask around it so that the light could not be seen from above.

There were a number of code words used to advise signalmen of impending air raids: on air raid warning 'red' the signalman had to stop any train approaching and inform the driver, who would endeavour not to open the firebox door unless absolutely necessary. GWR engines, which were exposed between the engine and tender, had a tarpaulin sheet between the two sections so as to prevent the glow showing when the fireman was shovelling coal into the firebox.

After eighteen months at Abbey Foregate I was promoted to porter signalman on the Shrewsbury to Welshpool line, at Hanwood, where we worked two shifts: 7.00am to 3.00pm and 2.00pm to 10.00pm. Among my weekly duties I had to clean and trim the seven-day signal lamps, and take them to the signal posts.

Each day small parcels arrived for local delivery by the railway. These were called 'paid home', for which we received 6d a parcel. In addition, on every Friday evening up to twenty pigeon fanciers with more than 100 pigeons arrived from the local Hanwood-Portesbury Pigeon Club. The birds each had a ring put on one leg before they were placed in a basket. Then later, as each of the birds arrived home, these rings were removed and placed in the special pigeon clock to ascertain the winner. Meanwhile, I had to weigh each basket, charge the appropriate price and stick the parcel stamp with the value on the basket before loading them all on the 6.30pm Aberystwyth to Shrewsbury train, en route to their destination.

Shrewsbury was noted for its butter market, where many local farmers and smallholders displayed and sold their produce. One such smallholder was called Mrs Davies. She lived at Hanwood and would frequently go to Brimingham beforehand, by train, and purchase up to ten boxes of apples, vegetables and crates of live chickens at the open-air market in the Bull Ring, where prices were somewhat lower. She would then return several hours later and, after her purchases had been unloaded from the train by the station porters, leave it to her somewhat diminutive husband to remove everything to their home, using a pony and trap: invariably, this would take him no less than five trips!

On 9 June 1946 I was made redundant at Hanwood as Harry Nightingale, a drum major with the King's Shropshire Light Infantry, returned from the army and took over from me, after a period of training. I was then sent to Admaston Station as a signalman Grade 4. This box, on the main line near Wellington, had just five levers, and I replaced Charles Jones, who was promoted to Class 3 at Wellington No 1 box. Unfortunately, he found that he was on the same shift as his father at Wellington No. 2, a higher class, and as he was still living at home he found the endless conversation about railway rules and regulations more than he could stomach. As a result, he asked for his old job back, and on 13 August of that year I was again made redundant.

I then did temporary relief work, mostly as a porter at Walcot Station, between Shrewsbury and Wellington, in Shropshire. Then, on 1 January 1947, I began my main signalling career at Marsh Farm Junction, situated between Marsh Brook and Craven Arms on the Shrewsbury to Hereford line. This was the junction on the line to Much Wenlock, again in Shropshire and known as Mary Webb's country; she was the author of *Gone to Earth* and other books.

I remained a signalman for the next nineteen years in Herefordshire, Shropshire and both mid– and central–Wales, working a total of 41 signal boxes. They included the 180-lever Severn Bridge Junction, the largest semaphore signalbox now in operation. During that period I personally knew a number of signalmen who, for various reasons, such as lack of concentration or insufficient sleep before a night shift, made mistakes which resulted in simple derailments or far more serious accidents. In many ways this was not altogether surprising, especially when a signalman was working on his own in a country signalbox, with only oil lamps for illumination and no visual aids such as track circuits (an electrical means by which the presence of a train outside was indicated in the signalbox) to assist him.

In those early days freight trains had no continuous brakes between the engine and the wagons, the only brake being on the steam engine, although there was a handbrake in the guard's brakevan at the rear. On certain sections of line these freight trains could comprise up to 100 wagons, and the only means of communication between the driver and guard was by handsignals, flags or lamps. However, strict compliance with the rules and regulations helped to combat any shortcomings in the system.

As always, time passes by, and as I, and others like me, grew up on the railway, so the railways also grew up! For my part, I was, in 1962, appointed a traffic regulator (inspector) at Gloucester Central GWR East box. Here, there were two stations, one GWR and the other LMS: until 1965 they were independent, each with its own stationmaster and separate administration department. My main responsibilities were to regulate the very heavy movements of freight trains through the area en route to and from South Wales, the Midlands and the North. The principal train of the day was known as the *Cheltenham Flyer*, which arrived from Cheltenham hauled by a GWR tank engine. A GWR 'Hall' class engine would then be attached to the rear, and the train would depart for Paddington at 8.00am, calling at Stroud and Kemble en route. It was a 'black mark' for anyone who delayed this train. Regrettably, during my first week on the early shift, I miscalculated the length of the preceding freight train, which was to stand and take water on the through line. As a result, I was unable to platform the *Cheltenham Flyer* and it was delayed six minutes: Mr Shaw, the stationmaster, was not amused!

In 1965, thanks to Dr Beeching, I once more became redundant. I was then appointed to Bristol Temple Meads as a station inspector – by far the largest station with which I had been involved and quite daunting. The station itself was controlled by a signalbox at either end, both with over 300 miniature levers and with three signalmen in attendance. There were fifteen platforms and on my shift I was responsible for the 'upside' platforms (numbers 9 to 15), with a staff of four porters. In addition to being a busy passenger station, involving many engine changes, there were eight parcel trains during each 24-hour cycle and, as there is now, the 'up'/'down' postal and sleeper services. One day in the early 'eighties the 'up' sleeper caught fire when approaching Taunton, resulting in loss of life. Meanwhile, amongst the other passenger trains was the *Bristol Pullman*, a blue streamlined train and forerunner in design to the now popular 'Intercity' 125s.

Eighteen months later I was promoted to a higher grade inspector at Pilning, near the entrance to the Severn tunnel. There the duties included being propelled 'sitting' in a special guard's brakevan, equipped with two floodlights, into the Severn tunnel whenever something caused it to be closed. Once there, I then had to examine the line and remove whatever was causing an obstruction. Quite a spooky job, but I was still 'growing up' and learning.

In 1967 I was appointed as a relief signalling inspector for the West of England division, so I was at Swindon for the commencement of the major resignalling scheme for the division. This led, during the following year, to the opening of a modern power signalbox, worked by three signalmen on each shift and covering a distance of some 45 miles. It also dispensed with seventeen manual signalboxes, making redundant the three men per box, as well as the relief signalmen.

A similar scheme followed shortly afterwards at Gloucester, where I was the operating department's representative at its inception. There were four signalmen per shift in the power box, covering an area from Lydney and Berkeley Road to Bromsgrove, via Gloucester. Unfortunately, this meant the closing of thirty signalboxes and the end of a way of life for many signalmen.

Bristol's new power signalbox, by far the biggest of its day, was next on stream, opening in 1971. Forty-nine signalboxes were closed on this occasion, as the Bristol area extended westwards to the outskirts of Taunton. I was appointed as a traffic supervisor in Bristol signalbox and remained there for the next eight years, before changing direction on appointment to chief trains' inspector. This was mainly passenger and freight train working, training and examining guards, shunters and other station staff from Penzance to Gloucester and Westbury on their knowledge of rules and regulations. My team comprised seventeen inspectors based throughout the Westcountry, and we were selected to introduce the 'open station concept', ie no ticket examination at entrance or exit barriers. This was a major scheme and involved much training to teach and motivate guards and ticket staff, who, like ourselves, had little confidence in such a scheme.

Then, on 9 January 1983, I was requested to transfer to Exeter as the operating manager. This covered an area from Totnes to Taunton, as well as from Barnstaple and Sherbourne on the Waterloo line, and included a staff of over 400. The resignalling of the Exeter area followed: this was completed in 1988, just on my retirement.

As the chief inspector and operations manager, my duties sometimes also involved meeting with members of the Royal Family, including The Princess of Wales at Heathfield and The Prince at Totnes, travelling on the royal trains to various locations.

Signalling has come a long way from 'bus line phones', lonely signalmen, and oil lamps, although I still have some oil signal lamps at home and I often reminisce about my life on the railway.

Mr David Evans' father, David Glasfryn Evans, was employed as a signalman at Moretonhampstead Station for many years up until the line from Newton Abbot was closed to passengers in March 1959, and is shown in the photograph below standing outside the signal box. Taken on 14 February 1959, the photograph also shows Horace Floyd, a local coal merchant, unloading a truck on the siding leading to the engine shed, upon the side of which the signal box was built:–

David W. Evans

✳✳✳✳✳

7. PORTER

Pat, the oldest in a family of eleven, writes of the fond memories she has of her father, who spent all his working life on the railway:–

When I awoke on the morning of 2 January 1970, little did I think that this was to prove one of the saddest days of my life, for at 1 o'clock that afternoon my dear dad (aged 62) died from a heart attack, in the Royal Devon and Exeter Hospital. His death was as unexpected as it was shocking, but the heart attack was no doubt triggered by the persistent cough which had troubled him for some time.

My father, who had worked on the Southern Railway as a 'uniform man' for over forty years, was not only a railwayman but also a walking railway encyclopedia. His official job title was 'Relief Parcel Porter', but during his many years of service he carried out, in a relief capacity, almost every type of job that the railway had to offer, including work as a guard, stationmaster, leading porter, ticket collector and level crossing keeper. On numerous occasions he was also offered promotion to an administrative post, but such promotion would have meant his leaving Exeter to set up home in another part of the country. This apart, he preferred to work out in the open: office work had little appeal. There was also my dear mother and a wonderful family of eleven children to consider, for I was the oldest of six daughters and I had five brothers: my oldest brother also worked on the Southern Railway.

My father was the most conscientious of employees and dedicated to his work. I have said that he was a 'uniform man', and he was indeed that, from head to toe. He kept his work clothes in immaculate condition, and whenever I saw a pair of brightly polished boots on the 'Cherry Blossom' advertisements, I always thought of my dad: he even used boot polish to shine the peak of his cap. His buttons, meanwhile, were cleaned to perfection with 'Brasso'. He was not a tall man, but he was dapper and, when he

71

went off to work in his smart peaked cap, jacket with polished buttons, sharp creased trousers and shining boots, you were looking at a man who was happy in his work and clearly took pride in it: he was a credit to the Southern Railway.

This fact did not go unnoticed by the powers that be either, for when any new people were taken on you could be sure that some of the time in their early days was always spent with my dad. Under his watchful eye, they quickly became familiar with the many complex facets of working on the railway. Some of the young men who passed through his hands went on to become managers themselves in other parts of the region, and, some even returned to Exeter in senior positions.

When off-duty, dad would still look as smart as ever in his civvy clothes. On a Thursday night he would make tracks for the railway club and, with his mates, relax over a few beers and enjoy a game of billiards. In fact, he was a useful player and won several medals for his prowess.

Dressed in his navy blue suit and wide-brimmed trilby hat, dad bore a striking resemblance to the Hollywood film actor George Raft. There, however, the similarity to him (or at least his screen image) ended, because George Raft always played gangsters or villains whereas my dad, bless him, was a family man with a great sense of humour and a love of music, being a competent pianist. His wages on the railway were, by today's standards, miserly to say the least. Immediately prior to his death, his basic pay was only £14 a week, and, with my dear mother and eleven children to support, overtime payments were a crucial element of the family budget. This meant that he worked long arduous shifts, necessitating, perhaps, an early rise at 4.30am or not returning home until 7.00am, after a night shift.

Today the world of steam and, in particular, steam engines is looked upon with affectionate nostalgia, and rightly so. However, the environment in which my father, and others like him, had to work was one of steam, smoke and soot, day in and day out, which could hardly have been conducive to good health. Today's Health and Safety at Work legislation and the railway of yesteryear would have been somewhat incompatible!

As far as our family life was concerned we were, on the whole, as children, pretty well behaved. Well, at least, I like to think so! If things did start to get out of hand, dad would sometimes blow his guard's whistle, after which peace and quiet would resume.

Apart from being eternally grateful to my dad for all that he did to care for us as a family, I know that he would be the first to acknowledge and pay tribute to my dear mother, who, happily, is still alive and who, in those days of raising a large family on a very low income, carried out the task with total dedication. We lived in a modest and, thanks to my mother, a well-kept home: a terraced house with three upstairs bedrooms, a nice, but rarely used, front room, a middle room, used as a fourth bedroom (for mum and dad), a breakfast room and a scullery.

Mum and dad ran a 'tight ship' – they had to – but we were brought up to respect the proper values required to live a life of love and service.

A view of Exeter Central Station on 21 August 1954 showing (in the foreground) No. 30676, an 0–4–4T of the 'M7' class, leaving on a train of LSWR stock for Exmouth.

Peter W. Gray

❋❋❋❋❋

8. CLERICAL WORKER

Mr Leslie King was born in 1912, the son of a post office clerk at Cullompton, but has now retired to Felixstowe. Most of his working life was spent on the railway and he was one of the few selected for the GWR Special Training Scheme (1921 – 1939):–

I went to a church school when I was 3¹/₂ years old and remained there until I won a scholarship to Tiverton Boys Middle School, in 1923. Unfortunately, only about four years later, my mother contracted TB, and it was then that I decided that I would join the GWR so as 'to get a job with a pension at sixty': a pension was considered very important in those days

When I left school in the summer of 1927, I started work at Hele

Hele & Bradninch Station, on the main line between Exeter and Taunton, where Leslie King started work on the railway as an unpaid learner junior clerk at the age of 15. Although this photograph was taken some 30 years later, on 5 August 1957, as ex-GWR 4–6–0 No. 6021 *King Richard II* thunders through on the 'up' line at the head of the 6.25am express from Penzance to Paddington, the station is still in its original form.

Peter W. Gray

74

& Bradninch as an unpaid learner junior clerk. Then, after about three months, I was told: "Go to Bridgwater goods station for a permanent post – or get out". So, at the age of fifteen, I had to find lodgings – at a cost of 18/– (90p) a week out of a salary of £35 per annum – and knuckle down to work with no prospect of a holiday during the first year. The hours were from 9am to 6pm on weekdays, and from 9am to 1pm on Saturdays.

As I passed the annual examinations, so my salary rose to £45 and £55 respectively over the next two years. Then, at the age of eighteen, I had to go to Paddington in order to take a special examination. Once again, I was successful and this led to my being appointed to a permanent job as a clerk at Bridgwater goods station – on a salary of £80 per annum, and with annual increments rising to £210 per annum at the age of thirty-one: this was the maximum for Class 5, compared to a goods manager's salary of £1,000 per annum.

There were few opportunities to break into Class 4 and above, and to become 'Special Class' was but a dream. Consequently, I attended night school in Bridgwater – typing, shorthand and bookkeeping – and went to St John's Ambulance classes etc. I also joined the Youth Hostel Association when it started in the 'thirties: free railway tickets gave me opportunities to travel in the UK and on the Continent.

Out of the blue, in 1934, I was appointed personal clerk to the district goods manager at Exeter and, on his recommendation, was subsequently given the opportunity to become a 'Special Trainee', starting a three-year programme in January 1937. This meant, first of all, going to the various Great Western goods stations in London, then to Cardiff district for six months and, finally, to the Birmingham goods manager's office for a further six months before moving to the chief goods manager's office at Paddington.

Shortly afterwards, in 1939, the Second World War began, but although I registered for active service I was not called up as I was in a reserved occupation, trains being essential for transport. Instead, with four other trainees, I went to cover vacancies at Bridgwater goods station for a while and was then directed to act as goods agent at Malvern Link, busy with military activity. However, after only four more months I received a telephone call telling me to: "Drop everything and report to Exeter district goods manager's office to shadow the chief clerk". This fateful decision led to me being bombed out of my home in Exeter during one of the air raids on the city, but later, after setting up home again in

Cullompton, it also resulted in my being appointed chief clerk in the DGMO.

Nationalisation, in 1948, included the GWR at Exeter taking over 38 former Southern Railway stations, and Plymouth taking over the balance west of Exeter. Seven years later all this was effectively reversed! Obviously, by then, the whole railway system was in a mess financially, physically, politically and psychologically. Profit became a byword (the GWR had paid a 4.5% dividend on ordinary stock in 1938).

When, in 1963, a division was set up at Plymouth (a shocking waste of somebody's money) I became sales office superintendent there, but this was short-lived as not long after the whole outfit folded; then I became field sales manager, with twelve salesmen, in the Bristol divisional organisation.

In short, I was but one of the army of railwaymen in retreat – doomed by the motor car, the express bus and coach, the aeroplane, the relatively short distances of our island and the effect of two world wars. Virtually everything was run down or outdated: we had invented railways, but for practical purposes they had had their day.

When I began work there had been over a hundred private companies, with revenues divided by the railway clearing house in Eversholt Street, London. Today, I think, there are around 25: how they divide receipts and expenditure and sort out their accounts is a matter for speculation.

I saw the 'writing on the wall' years ago! Domestic considerations dominated my decision to get out at the age of 57, leading to a long and happy retirement in Felixstowe. I still derive benefit from the pension which cost 5% of my salary in the distant yesterdays.

The former special trainees are now down to ten. The 68th annual reunion took place in April 1998, reflecting the *esprit de corps* of the GWR.

Looking back, I can recognise the qualities of the men with whom I worked as a lad, fellows who had survived the battlefields of France and the perilous sea – cynical, tough, decent, full of fun; some bitter, but all accepting the hard terms of a profit-making company. I am indebted to those who made possible my special training, men of tough experience and character. After nationalisation other regions were unenthusiastic about GWR men; we were in the lead in so many ways, hence their tag 'God's

Wonderful Railway'. Moreover, until nationalisation, our shareholders had received dividends: many others had not.

The GWR secured its financial objectives, and enabled me to achieve mine.

Mr Alec Bowditch, the youngest of a family of five (three boys and two girls), was among the many people facing the difficulty of finding employment in the 'threadbare 'thirties':–

I left school in the winter of 1934 when I was fourteen years old. It was not an ideal time to find a job, rather like the early 'nineties: regular work was at a premium, with a large pool of people on the dole. Nevertheless, I managed to find odd jobs for three months and then applied for the post of lad messenger at the goods department of the Great Western Railway at Taunton. My brothers, George and Jack, who were seventeen and sixteen years older than I respectively, had both commenced employment in this capacity at the same depot when they were my age: at the time of my application they were both motor drivers.

My interview took place in the office of the goods agent, a Mr F. L. Angle – a rather stern, but softly spoken gentleman. He tested my ability to answer questions on a general knowledge basis. This was then followed by a session of questions about the geography of the British Isles; writing and spelling tests came next, with Mr Angle reading an article from a newspaper at a slow speed for me to record on paper. The interview finished with the usual phrase of "there are others to be interviewed: we will be in touch".

Having two brothers as employees at the depot must have counted in my favour, for in the course of time I was informed that I was to be offered the position on a temporary basis for a period of six months. If I proved a 'likely lad' I would be considered for regular employment, provided that I passed the railway doctor's examination (at my expense!).

I first walked into the general office of the goods department at Canal Road, Taunton on 18 March 1935, with more than a little misgiving. The hours of employment were 8.00am to 5.30pm, Mondays to Fridays, with one hour for lunch, and 8.00am to 1.30pm on Saturdays, making a total of 48 hours a week for a wage of 15/– (75p), minus deductions. For the first two days I was shown the ropes by another lad messenger, then I was on my own. Apart from my list of duties, which was considerable, I was expected to answer the two telephones. In the main, the calls were enquiries from traders and district office, Exeter. There was also a 'wall phone' which connected the goods department with other local departments and the telegraph department. Three rings received on the bell were answered by returning three, when someone was there to speak. The telegraph office was also used for sending messages in railway code to other depots within the British Isles.

I had no previous experience of answering telephones and, at first, I was terrified. There were about fifteen clerks in the general office and it took me some time to learn all their names. At that time all clerks had to be addressed as 'Mr'. Mostly they were an understanding bunch and did what they could to help the new lad; others, though, stood on ceremony and were very aloof.

The first job of the day was the opening of envelopes which had arrived by the railway companies' own system and were known as 'train letters'. This was a time-consuming job: each piece of correspondence had to be smoothed out and endorsed with a date stamp. The sorting of outwards invoices in alphabetical order as well as by railway company order also took a lot of time. Filing of correspondence and then connecting incoming letters to their particular reference was also the 'boy's job'.

After lunch it was all go once again: most of the afternoon was spent with the despatch of 'train letters', all of which had to be addressed by me. Responsibility for the 'stamp registers' ($1/2$d, 1d, and $11/2$d) for mail to be sent by post was also part of my job, and they had to be maintained meticulously; if they did not balance I would find myself on the mat in front of the chief clerk!

Geography had been one of my favourite subjects at school, and railway work added to my meagre knowledge of the subject. Most of the text for 'phone messages from the telegraph officer would be in the parlance of the 'Railway Telegraph Code Book'. All the rivers of the world seemed to be part of the code and each had its specific meaning – Moselle: 'give matter special attention'; Tagus: 'following hence today'; Rhone: 'your communication of date'; Ohio: 'send with all speed' were just some. The work of the office boy was no sinecure and it was always said that a fully-trained boy in a Great Western office was well on the way to becoming a clerical unit.

In the five-and-a-half years of my lad messenger's service I did have some variation of work. For about a year I was asked to cover the duties of the weighbridge lad porter, which meant that I had to deal with members of the general public as well as our own motor carmen and horse carmen. Coal merchants, scrap metal men, banana importers, hide and skin merchants and even the local constabulary, with vehicles suspected of being overloaded, all came to the weighbridge.

My railway career was brought to a temporary halt by the outbreak of the Second World War, in 1939. For a short while before joining up I was a member of the Railway Home Guard, known then as the LDV (Local Defence Volunteers). We were sent out to guard railway bridges in the area: three men armed with one revolver and three rounds of ammunition formed a patrol! The next five-and-a-half years were spent in the Royal Air Force, where I received training as a motor driver and, in the process, saw the Middle East at the expense of the British government.

My RAF service ended in May 1946. Whilst on demobilisation leave I made one or two visits to the Taunton goods depot, and during one such visit I was persuaded by the goods agent to make myself available for work. I was hopeful that I would be employed in a clerical position, but there was opposition to this and, instead, I started back as a temporary relief motor driver. Prior to taking the wheel of a GWR road vehicle, I had to pass a test conducted by a member of the district road motor engineer's staff. This obstacle overcome, I was sent to outlying stations to deliver and collect traffic from the company's customers.

Much of this work entailed delivery of fertilisers, basic slag and feeding-stuffs to farms. In fact, I spent three months of that autumn based at the small station at Dunster, on the Minehead branch line, delivering such traffic to farms high on Exmoor. The GWR's lorry fleet was, in the main, of early 1930s vintage and nigh on 'clapped out'. However, it was expected that it would be some time before new vehicles became available and so it was a question of doing the best we could with the tools we had.

My vehicle at Dunster was an 'A1' type Thornycroft 3-ton flat lorry. Loaded with fertiliser for the Exmoor farms, I found it a very hard job to coax the lorry to climb the hills in the locality. A water can, fully-charged, was always in the cab, and half way up the hill leading to the 'Rest and be Thankful' inn, at Wheddon Cross, the radiator would be boiling. Consequently, I would have to pull in and top up the radiator after allowing the water to cool. However, it was quite an enjoyable time; life was much more relaxed and, as long as we did our job to their satisfaction, no-one bothered us.

I continued as a motor driver until September 1950, mostly at Taunton goods depot. The GWR considered their motor drivers to be ambassadors for the company, as they had the first and last contact with the customer. Politeness at all times was the rule, and some very special relationships were made and maintained, ensuring that satisfaction was given and custom retained.

For about eighteen months I operated a country lorry service from Taunton goods depot, covering the Quantock and Blackdown Hills on alternate days. This was a very busy life, delivering both passenger and goods traffic: PLA (passenger luggage in advance) was very popular with holiday folk and also with pupils attending boarding schools and colleges. Whilst covering those hill villages I also 'delivered' the local news, remembering to be tactful at all times, and was never short of a cup of tea or cocoa. In fact, some of the farmers' wives, on seeing the lorry pull into the farmyard, would have a cuppa ready in no time at all and a slice of home-made cake to accompany it. One cold morning, when I called at a country cottage, I was even offered a glass of something 'warming', which turned out to be parsnip wine: this almost took the breath out of me, but certainly warmed the morning most pleasantly!

Although still a member of the 'uniform' staff, for short periods during 1948/9 I was called upon at Taunton goods depot to assist with clerical duties. During my final days with the RAF I had been employed on such duties within the motor transport section, but the GWR tradition demanded that a clerical examination be taken prior to transfer from the uniform to a clerical position. Consequently, in late 1949, I sat the exam at Exeter and was told, at a much later date, that I had been accepted for clerical duties. It was not to be in my home town of Taunton, however. District office, Exeter, instructed me to report to the stationmaster at Langport West for a position in the goods office.

In those days Langport was a very busy station, employing five staff in the goods office and one in the booking office. For the next three-and-a-half years I spent some very happy times there. Bill Teague, a Devonian from Bovey Tracey, was the stationmaster. He was a very friendly and understanding man, and well-respected by his staff. I travelled to Langport on the 6.50am train each weekday, returning on the 4.30pm service. In those days we also had to work a half day on Saturdays.

In 1953 I was transferred back to Taunton goods department, where both my brothers were supervisory foremen. My job was in the claims section dealing with demands from the general public for loss or damage to their goods. It was very interesting work, and I found myself involved with claims, in various forms, for almost the rest of my working life. However, I realised that I had to obtain work outside of the Taunton area if I wished to gain promotion, which was very slow in those days.

In June 1961 I was made a claims investigator at the divisional manager's office in Bristol. This did not mean that I had to move my home: being a divisional appointment, I was expected to travel anywhere between Swindon and Penzance on investigations. It was prior to Dr Beeching's cutbacks, and for the next two years I travelled on some of the delightful branch lines that were soon to be closed, including those to Kingsbridge (from Brent), Tavistock, (from Plymouth North Road) and Tiverton, and beyond (on the lovely Exe Valley line). In addition, I covered all of the branch lines in Cornwall, which now, sadly, are but memories in most instances.

The start of the Beeching era saw me back in uniform when I was made a claims prevention inspector at Exeter, which, at that time, was a 'day to day' office under the control of the newly created Plymouth division. My brother, Jack, had been promoted in 1957 to be a cartage & terminals inspector at the office of the district goods manager, so my move to Exeter meant that we saw much more of one another: both of us were domiciled in Taunton and, if going to the office, travelled together. However, before long, more changes were afoot, and between 1965 and 1969 my base was shifted no less than three times: to Reading, to Paddington and then to Bristol, on promotion to chief inspector of the National Carriers HQ at St Lawrence House. Finally, in 1974, when many of the staff at the National Carriers HQ were relocated, I took up a clerical post (later becoming supervisor) at Taunton goods depot and remained there until being made redundant in 1979, when I was almost 60 years old.

In all, the three Bowditch brothers gave almost 150 years service to the railway transport industry as George, my eldest brother, had spent all of his working life at Taunton goods depot, having retired from his post as senior supervisor in 1968. He had also been a JP and, in his final year with the industry, had been honoured in the Queen's Awards. Sadly, I am now the only survivor, and I look back on the days with the railways when it was a pleasure to go to work. Camaraderie of the old railwaymen had to be experienced to be believed.

Yes, railways were a family concern with the Bowditch's. My father's brother, Alf, was a permanent way inspector at Newton Abbot in the 1930s, his son, Fred, was a telegraph clerk at Birmingham, Paddington and Taunton, and his other son, Leslie, was a relief stationmaster in the Plymouth division and remembered, I expect, by some of the 'old sweats'.

The Bowditch brothers – (*Left to right*) George – Alec – Jack – who, collectively, gave almost 150 years service to the railway transport industry.

Alec Bowditch

Mr Douglas Charles Croker was born on 31 May 1902: now well into his nineties, he still has an agile brain and can recollect in detail his employment with the GWR. When he was 21 he was awarded 'Excellent, 95%' for an essay he wrote on *Healthy Ambitions*. I quote an extract: 'One of the most important habits to be cultivated is discipline for, until a man knows how to obey, he cannot attain that power of command without which no efficient working can be accomplished. Tidiness is another habit which cannot be formed too early, not only does this stand for neat and methodical working, but it is a big time-saver. The habit of courtesy is also a great asset; it often requires some effort to be courteous, but this effort is never lost. Lastly, probably the most important habit is that of being thorough; discipline, tidiness and courtesy will be of little avail if a youth does his work in a careless slipshod manner'.

When I left school in the summer of 1917 the First World War meant that the choice of work was limited. I did not want to join my father, who was a master baker, so, instead, I applied for work as a clerk with the Great Western Railway. My grandfather had worked as a signalman at Teignmouth before retiring in 1893.

Having completed the application form and provided the three necessary testimonials (including one from my headmaster), I was summoned to Exeter to sit for the entrance examination. I passed that, and also the medical examination: the fee of 5/– (25p) for the latter was subsequently deducted from my first salary payment.

On Monday, 28 September 1917 I began work as a junior clerk at Taunton goods department. Condition 4 on the application form stated that 'a junior clerk, if not residing with his parents or relatives, must satisfy the Company that he is suitably lodged'. I found such lodgings and was able to return home to Bridgwater, 11 miles away, at weekends. However, as my starting salary of £25 per annum did not cover the cost of 12/– (60p) a week for lodgings (washing not included) and some pocket money, my parents had to subsidise me until I received my first increase of £10 per annum at the end of the first year. I enjoyed working with the office staff, who were kind and understanding, and, fortunately, we were not involved in the railway strike from 27 September to 5 October 1919.

When I was aged 18 I had to apply for senior status, which was dependent on passing an examination at Paddington. I failed by four marks on my first attempt, but succeeded the second time. Much emphasis was laid on arithmetic and, as I later became involved in accountancy, I could see why this was important. Shorthand, incidentally, was an optional subject for the entrance examination.

Taunton goods department staff, c1920:–
Top row (left to right) – Mr A. Savage, D. Croker, E. Runnides, J. Gardner, Miss L. Sweet, Mr Shipway (chief clerk), G. Garland.
Bottom row – Harold Potter, Mr T. Pape, Mr Brannan.

Douglas Croker

At very short notice I was informed, on a Friday in January 1921, that I was to report to the Exeter goods agent on the following Monday. Fortunately, I had a friend working there and he was able to get me fixed up in his lodgings without difficulty.

After working at Exeter goods station, I was transferred to the district traffic manager's office, dealing mainly with station correspondence. I preferred station work, so in 1928 I applied for a transfer and was sent to Dulverton goods station, in Somerset, a very busy little place. Timber, grown in the area, was an important revenue-earning commodity. The senders provided measurement specifications, and it was the job of the goods clerk to convert them into tonnage for rate-charging purposes. This was an intricate and time-consuming procedure.

Other goods were delivered by the one lorry and driver to a wide area of Exmoor, made very difficult in winter by fog, frost and snow. During the hunting season the loading and unloading of horses also provided a lucrative source of income.

After a few months I arranged, in October 1928, an exchange with a clerk at Tiverton Station. I was fortunate in finding good lodgings whilst I looked for a flat, so that I could marry my fiancée. Later we were able to buy our own house in Tiverton, where our son was born. In due course he attended Blundell's School as a day boy.

Tiverton Station on 3 December 1929, after heavy rain had caused the nearby River Lowman to burst its banks.

Douglas Croker

Much of the traffic at the station was composed of products from J. Heathcoat & Co's factory, although poultry and rabbits were despatched all the year round – and in greatly increased numbers in the weeks leading up to Christmas. Passengers luggage in advance (PLA), meanwhile, included that connected with Blundell's school at the beginning and end of each term as well as that connected with the Amory family, when they left for their hunting lodge at Pitlochry, in Scotland. In both instances, the amounts of luggage were so vast that relief porters had to be engaged to help cover the extra work.

The booking office was also kept very busy during the football season (when fans travelled to see the Exeter City football team playing at St James's Park), during the summer months (when half-day excursions and evening trips were run to the seaside towns of Dawlish, Teignmouth and Paignton) and again during the Christmas period (when there were trips to Exeter for shopping and pantomimes), such trips by rail being extremely popular in the years before road traffic took over.

Mr G. Hulme, the stationmaster, with the clerks, Douglas Croker and Len Wellington, and the permanent way gang at Tiverton Station in 1935.

Douglas Croker

When the Second World War began there was a great influx of troops to the town, the first being the Somerset Light Infantry. As I was in a reserved occupation I was exempt from military service, but I joined the Home Guard from its beginning until it was disbanded at the end of the war.

During the early stages of the war, troops were granted weekend leave and, as many of the men lived in Somerset, there was quite a rush at around mid-day on Saturdays, when the booking office staff would be taxed to the utmost: most of the tickets had to be written out by hand, no printed stock being available.

There were many difficulties during the war, but, with the coming of D-Day, and the threat of invasion rapidly receding, many of the beaches that had previously been closed were re-opened. This, in turn, placed a lot of pressure on the Paddington booking office staff and resulted in my being moved there and having to make the necessary journey on Sunday, 13 August 1944. My first job on arriving for duty was to bundle up the large number of treasury notes that the booking office staff had not had time to sort. Meanwhile, my sleeping accommodation was in the Underground shelters and I had my meals either at Lyon's shop in Praed Street, where I paid 1/2d (6p) for breakfast, or in the city, where lunch usually cost 2/3d (11p). A haircut, incidentally, cost 1/6d (7½p). I also remember that on one of my off-duty walks in the city I had to take shelter from a German V2 rocket bomb!

Only a few days after arriving in London, however, my son had to have an operation in Tiverton Hospital, and I was allowed to return home on the Thursday evening. I then travelled all night in a train which was so crowded that I, like many others, had to stand squashed in the corridor for the entire journey. Upon reflection, it seemed strange that I, a married man with a family, had been sent to London in preference to the single man who replaced me.

I was very happy to be back in Tiverton and continued to enjoy both my work and the company of my colleagues up until I was successful in gaining promotion to the post of chief goods clerk, Class 4, at Cullompton Station on 9 January 1945. This followed the introduction of the advertising of clerical vacancies covering the whole of the GWR system and meant that I could travel daily from Tiverton. Later I was upgraded to Class 3, when the work there increased.

Once the railways had been nationalised in 1948 there were many changes, but I remained at Cullompton until being promoted to chief goods clerk Class 2, at St Austell. By that time, my family and I had moved from Tiverton to Exeter and, as we were still there, I was allowed home every two weeks. This, of course, meant a lot of travelling, and, on one occasion, the sea was so rough that it was washing over the railway line between Dawlish and Teignmouth. As it was considered unsafe the line was closed temporarily and trains were diverted from Plymouth to Exeter via the Southern Railway through Tavistock and Okehampton. Needless to say, I was very late arriving home that particular weekend!

When the Bridgwater chief goods clerk's post became vacant I applied for a transfer on compassionate grounds. My elderly parents lived in Bridgwater and my father was very ill, which made things difficult for my mother. Also, our son had moved to Reading on his first teaching post, so my wife was on her own. The outcome was that I moved there on 3 January 1955 and was later upgraded to Class 1.

The Bridgwater goods agent was also the dockmaster as the docks at Bridgwater, and the wharf at Dunball, were owned by the railway. Imports consisted of timber, grain, fertilisers and other commodities: it was one of my regular duties to arrange the supply of crane drivers at each place. In addition, because Bridgwater was a busy industrial town, much other business came to the railway, an aspect particularly noticeable when the Hinckley Point Power Station was built as much of the building material was dealt with at the station.

In 1966 the old Somerset & Dorset line was closed under the Beeching axe, so the stationmaster at Glastonbury was without a job. As he was in the same grade as myself, and I was nearing the age of 64, I was offered early retirement, with a 'Golden Handshake'. This was accepted and I ended my long and interesting railway career on 31 May 1966.

Sadly, by that time, a number of other lines had also fallen under the Beeching axe, including the Exe Valley and the Tiverton to Tiverton Junction lines. However, at least the people of Tiverton, where I had spent so many happy years, will always have a reminder of the railway, because Lord Amory purchased one of the little steam engines (affectionately called the 'Tivvy Bumper') that regularly worked trains in the area and presented it to the town. The locomotive, 14XX class No. 1442, was then exhibited in Blundells Road (opposite the goods yard) until later being removed to the covered 'Railway Gallery' in the excellent Tiverton Museum, in St Andrew's Street.

Miss Joyce Bond was born in Cardiff, in September 1922, and the railway has been part of her life ever since:-

When I was born, my father was employed as a head shunter in the goods department of the Great Western Railway in Cwmbran, near Cardiff. Less than a year later, though, my grandfather became ill and this led to my father applying for a transfer to Tiverton Station, and to the family home being moved to Bickleigh, from where my parents had originated.

Later, as I grew up, I attended Bickleigh School and, from there, moved on to Tiverton Girls Middle School, where I passed the Oxford School Certificate in 1939. At that time I was also due to take the Civil Service examination, but when war was declared on 3 September the exam was cancelled and it looked as if I was destined to continue in a (non-railway) job as a junior clerk that had been arranged for me by my school. However, in the meantime, men were being called up into the armed forces, among them many from the GWR, so there were increasing numbers of vacancies for women to replace them. Moreover, one such vacancy occurred in the booking office at Tiverton Station and, on seeing the post being advertised, I applied and was subsequently accepted.

As soon as I started the job, in July 1941, I was made to feel welcome by everyone, and the senior booking clerk, who had been working at the station since 1923, went on to teach me accountancy and all about passenger and parcels work. Looking back, I was very fortunate that I had such a kind, efficient and patient gentleman to work with, and shall always be grateful for what he did. The working conditions, too, were satisfactory, and the fact that I was mostly with men – the other women at the station were employed in the goods office – caused no problems at all. Much the same applied to having to work different shifts on alternate weeks, as this was something to which I soon grew accustomed: the hours were from 7.30am to about 4.00pm for one week, with a half day on Saturday, and from 9.00am or 10.00am to about 7.00pm or 7.30pm, with a half day on Thursday, for the next. In addition, because there was a Sunday service from Tiverton to Dawlish Warren (and other stations through to Paignton) during June, July and August, the booking office staff were also involved in Sunday working rosters for several weeks throughout the summer.

In those days most people in Tiverton and the surrounding district travelled by train, and local firms sent their goods by parcels or goods trains. In fact, the amount of traffic generated by the station was quite remarkable at times, but apart from being on the Exe Valley line (from Exeter St David's to Dulverton) it was, of course, also connected to Tiverton Junction and the main line beyond. To add to the workload, there were troops stationed in Tiverton during the war, who had to be issued with tickets when they went on leave. As far as I remember these included members of the Somerset Light Infantry, the Oxford & Bucks Regiment, the Devon & Somerset Regiment, the Devon & Dorset Regiment and the Women's Land Army. For a while, US army and navy personnel were also stationed in the town, some of whom took over a spare waiting room on the 'up' platform for use as a 'Railways Trains Office' (RTO); they often came to us for help with train services.

I had one sister in the Nursing Service and the other in the Women's Land Army, so we had a great get-together when they came home on leave. As I lived four miles from Tiverton, and the last train home was at 8.30pm, I could not take part in social events there, although there was an occasional dance in Bickleigh School. It must be remembered that people in villages were very isolated before the advent of cars and bus services, but I had (and still have) plenty of hobbies – knitting, dressmaking, reading and writing letters to friends – and I also enjoyed an occasional visit to cinemas in Tiverton. In addition, I often helped my father maintain a plot of land alongside the railway line at Cadeleigh Station (for Bickleigh) that he rented from the GWR for about 2/6d (12¹/₂p) a year: here, we grew all our own vegetables, which was a big help in wartime.

Cadeleigh Station on 8 July 1959, showing 0–6–0PT No. 7761 departing with its two-coach train on the 5.22pm Tiverton to Exeter service.

Peter W. Gray

During the war female staff were employed only on a temporary basis and paid weekly but, on 23 September 1946, I signed the admission form into the service of the Great Western Railway Company and was then employed on a permanent basis as a woman clerk, still at Tiverton booking office. At that time my weekly rate of pay was 46/– (£2.30), out of which I had to pay superannuation contributions and subscriptions to the Transport and Salaried Staff Association (TSSA). Meanwhile, most of the married women left as their husbands returned from the war and took up their positions once more, and the chief booking clerk, with whom I was working, gained promotion to chief goods clerk at Cullompton.

After the war Tiverton Station was still very busy, and nationalisation, in 1948, seemed to make no immediate difference. Certainly, so far as I was concerned, I continued to thoroughly enjoy my work, and the fact that women were restricted to certain grades only never bothered me; mostly, I agreed with that. I also continued to get on very well with all the other staff members around me and began to benefit, financially, from the introduction (in stages) of equal pay for women. This made me even happier!

In all, I spent 21 years at Tiverton until being promoted to budget clerk (Class 4) at Exeter St David's district staff office, in 1962. It was then very different, working in a large office with eight men, but, again, I was made to feel very welcome and this helped considerably. Soon after, though, came reorganisation, with the district office moving to Plymouth, and then to Bristol. I was transferred to the Exeter goods office but, as I was not very happy there, I applied for a grade to grade transfer to the Exeter St David's parcels accounts office. That, I found, was a much happier place in which to work.

When we took over all the accountancy of the Exeter district stations in 1966 I was upgraded to Class 3: I had always attended the TSSA Union meetings in Exeter and they had fought and won the case when my application had initially been turned down. Reorganisation, meanwhile, continued in all departments, but I did not get the relief clerk's post that I wanted because, at my interview, the area manager did not think that I should work on a night shift, if needed, when there were men in the goods department. At the time I was very annoyed and I told him so, too! That was also the only occasion on which being a female made any difference to me.

In 1976 I was presented with an engraved wristwatch on the completion of 35 years service and then, on 2 September of the following year, I retired, at the age of 55. Prior to this I had also passed examinations and received certificates for station accountancy (passenger and parcels) in 1953 and 1965, and for station accountancy (goods) in 1960. In addition, in 1954, I had obtained a certificate of merit for station accountancy (passenger and parcels).

Since retiring, I have been able to keep in touch with former colleagues from Exeter through regular retired staff reunions (all grades) at St George's Hall, Exeter, usually held in April each year. Also, as I am a life member of the BR-WR Retirement Association, I regularly receive information about pensions, staff travel restrictions and, latterly, the safeguarding of our pensions during privatisation.

There was a close comeraderie among employees wherever I worked during my many years on the railway, but things changed with all the reorganisation and I am glad that I took early retirement.

Mr Graham Freestone began his career on the railway at Exeter goods office in April 1948 and completed it at Exeter area manager's office, in various capacities:–

When I started work at Exeter virtually all goods traffic was carried by rail. At that time there were also four horses still in use in the goods yard, but, not long after my arrival, they were transferred to Bristol goods yard to complete their railway service, prior to retirement: I remember the day well because the stableman was in tears as his 'babies' were loaded ready for the journey.

Mechanical horses (scammels) had been in use for a number of years and were a great success on short journeys in and around the city. They were three-wheeled units which could attach a trailer already loaded by a checker and porter, and then be driven straight away to make the delivery. A carman (driver) could do up to four rounds a day instead of two.

One day, while I was at Exeter goods office, a train-load labelled 'ammunition' arrived in the yard, so the army was duly advised. Since they were unable to unload immediately, they provided an armed guard during the delay, only to find several days later that the wagon had been wrongly labelled and contained nothing more than office furniture. This caused much amusement!

In those days very few people owned cars, so almost all holiday-makers travelled by train. On Fridays the station buffet would remain open throughout the night as trains packed full of passengers for Devon and Cornwall arrived continuously.

During my time at Exeter goods office, King George VI and Queen Elizabeth paid a visit to Exeter, and I well remember the fish dock exit/entrance being cleaned thoroughly and the publicity department from Paddington coming down and transforming the area with flags, drapes etc., much like a stage set. There was little security compared to today's standards.

In April 1951 I applied, successfully, for a move to Cullompton, so as to broaden my railway experience. This proved to be a very happy posting and I soon immersed myself in a small town's activities. I had not been there long when a general election was due to take place, and I remember the goods foreman, Sid Bending, coming on duty early one morning and plastering 'VOTE FOR AMORY' (the Conservative candidate for Tiverton) posters all over the outside of the animal cake store. However, the storeman, Charlie Selwood, had extreme left-wing leanings, and when he arrived for work on the 8.10am train from Wellington he became enraged and insisted on every poster being removed immediately: being non-political, BR would have had them removed anyway. The unsuccessful Labour candidate was called Duffy and the local catchphrase was 'Don't let Duffy bluff ee'.

Some fairground owners had a base at Cullompton and caused a stir by sending some small bears by train. To keep them occupied they were given bottles of milk to drink. On another occasion the same people despatched some twenty fairground steam engines for scrap, which attracted a lot of local people to the station in order to take photographs or simply just to enjoy the sight. It was also whilst I was at Cullompton that tomatoes and cucumbers became widely available during the winter months (until then only obtainable in summer). Devon growers then began to send daily parcel vans to the markets of such places as London, Manchester and Birmingham.

When invoicing for 'smalls traffic' was abolished, my post was made redundant and I became a temporary district relief clerk, based at the district commercial manager's office at Exeter. During the five years that followed on relief I had many experiences, some sad, some happy, and some amusing. One of the sad days that I recall was when I was working at Bridgwater parcels office. On this particular day the office was very busy with outwards traffic, when an elderly man with a mac on his arm came into the office and asked about a train to Bristol. He then left and was seen, for some while after this, walking up and down the platform. In those days *The Cornishman* from Paignton to Wolverhampton passed through the station at about 3.30pm, and on this day it was forced to stop a mile or so beyond it, having hit a man who had fallen in front of the train. This was the man who had been into the office a short while before.

One of the ticket collectors at Bridgwater was very deaf and on one summer afternoon a passenger asked him if he knew the test score. He replied: "Next train: change at Weston".

At around mid-1954 the commercial aspects of the Southern Region west of Exeter were transferred to the Western Region, so relief clerks went to stations from Exeter Central to Okehampton, Barnstaple, Ilfracombe and Torrington. In those days, incidentally, it was quite common, if there was no porter available at some of them, for the clerk to have to clean out the grate and light his own fire.

I worked at Okehampton on many occasions and something of note usually happened. On one quiet afternoon, just after 2.00pm, a raft of wagons being moved from the military sidings to the goods yard became derailed, blocking all lines to the west of the station. Soon afterwards the *Atlantic Coast Express* arrived, very full as it included US sailors bound for Plymouth, with the result that I had to arrange buses locally as well as from Halwell, Bideford and Bude, whilst the stationmaster dealt with all the operating aspects. The lines were not cleared until after 8.00pm!

A few months later an old lady came to the parcels office in order to make arrangements for a dog to be sent away in a basket.

An unusual sight at Okehampton as 'T9' class 4–4–0 No. 120, in LSWR livery, heads a 'special' to Padstow on 21 April 1963. Approaching the station, from the Tavistock direction, is 'N' class 2–6–0 No. 31839 on a local service.

Mike Vinten

She then asked the parcels porter if she could take Fido for a walk before he went to this new home. He replied: "Yes, as long as you are back before the train arrives". In due course it came, and the porter looked out through the large window overlooking the street and said: "Where's that bloody old woman with the dog". A little voice behind him said: "Here I am"!

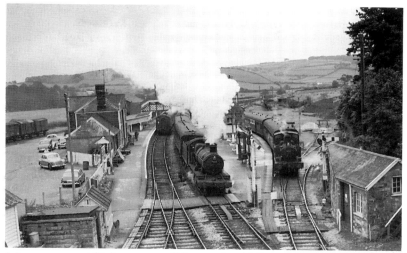

A busy scene at Dulverton on 7 September 1963 on 2–6–0 No. 7326 pulls out of the station with a Taunton to Barnstaple train (passing a Taunton-bound train in the process) and 0–4–2T No. 1450 waits in the 'back platform loop' before setting off for Exeter on the Exe Valley line.

Mike Vinten

In October 1960 I was promoted to Clerk 3 in the trains office of the district traffic operating office at Exeter. Immediately before taking up my new post, however, I was working at Dulverton at the time when Devon was suffering much damage through flooding. In fact, on my last day as a relief clerk the Exe Valley was extensively flooded all the way to Cadeleigh and there the railway looked as though it was going through a vast lake. Furthermore, the driver of the 6.00am push and pull train from Exeter to Dulverton, on which I was travelling, was forced to return to Exeter, where I later caught the 8.00am train bound for Taunton, hoping to get a connection from there to Dulverton. Alas, when I arrived at Taunton I found that there would be no train to Dulverton for at least an hour, so I strolled out into the street, only to find that that, too, was flooded as far as I could see. Eventually, though, I joined a train from Taunton to Barnstaple and finally reached Dulverton at 10.30am.

During the morning the floods at Tiverton gradually receded and the first train up the valley was expected at around 1.00pm. However, at 12.45pm, the control rang to say that both St David's and Cowley Bridge were flooded and that because the line at Cowley could be washed away within hours I was advised to leave for home on the next train. This I did, and managed to reach Stoke Canon without incident, only to find that all trains were being terminated there, with the possibility of buses to Exeter. The outcome was that I then had to wait about two hours until some high, open rear platform, double-decker buses arrived to begin conveying people from the various trains to Exeter and I eventually returned there shortly past 6.00pm – after the swell from the buses had thrown water up over the windows of the cottages in Stoke Canon and some had come inside the bus! But even then, despite having left home well over 12 hours earlier, there were still problems: the district of St Thomas, separated from Exeter by the River Exe, was now cut off and DUKWS (amphibious vehicles used in the war to transport soldiers on land and on water) of the Royal Marines had to be called in so that residents could be assisted to their homes.

My years in the trains office were very happy ones, despite the threats of closure from Dr Beeching. One of the amusing incidents was caused by the assistant district manager, Sam Squires, a man well known for referring to staff by their surname only. It was the practice of controllers to phone someone up and say: "Squires here; I want you in my office immediately". Most people knew who was phoning, but one day the real Sam Squires phoned and said: "Lavis, I want you in my office right away", to which Lavis replied: "Pull the other one" and put the 'phone down. But I think Sam Squires saw the funny side and nothing more happened.

My post eventually transferred to Plymouth so I opted for a vacancy in the rolling stock office, which was to remain at Exeter. It was then, or not long after I had settled into this completely new type of work and routine, that it was decided that with so many cars coming to the station and requiring parking spaces that a car park should be built. As the rolling stock office looked out on to a square containing wooden cottages (used by the works study team), a hut used for dancing classes and the old wartime control air raid shelter, it was decided to demolish all of these buildings so

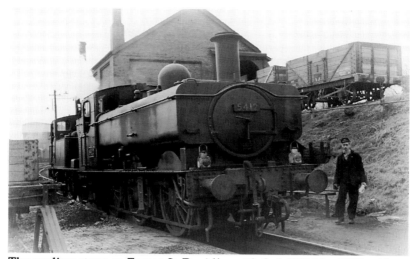

The coaling stage at Exeter St David's, with 0–6–0PT No. 5412 and an unidentified 0–4–2T of the '14XX' class standing on the coal road.

Mike Vinten

as to make way for the car park. However, this proved to be easier said than done. No problems arose with the cottage and hut, but the shelter was a different proposition altogether. As a result, it was decided that on a certain Sunday morning it would be detonated. The fuses were duly set and ignited with much noise, but the shelter remained undamaged, although the windows of many houses in the surrounding area were either cracked or blown out, including one of ours in the rolling stock office. Twice the army tried to blow it up with much stronger charges, without any success. Eventually, a heavy ball weight was brought in and repeatedly dropped on it, just chipping away small pieces at a time. It took many weeks to dispose of it!

Sadly the Exeter rolling stock office closed in September 1967 and I again found myself on district relief work, but this time it also meant relieving at Exeter Central, Exmouth, Honiton, Axminster and Chard Junction. However, that proved to be short-lived as on Christmas Eve that year we were told that our relief posts would be made redundant during 1968; thus in April 1968 I found myself as a relief clerk in the maintenance engineer's office at Newton Abbot. This was like embarking on an entirely new career, as I knew nothing of things mechanical. Surprisingly, though, I soon found myself rostering enginemen, ordering stock in the stores department and preparing bonus statements from engineering work slips, in both the carriage and wagon, and engine shops. On my first day in the carriage and wagon department I thought that I should never be able to cope with the noise, but I soon adjusted and did not even notice it. It took me many months, on the other hand, to begin to understand the enginemen's rosters, and the paybill work was quite different from paybills at passenger stations, having drivers' mileage payments, bonuses and completely different agreements for workshop staff. One very sad happening was when a fitter, the brother of English test cricketer Caldwell, was killed on duty in the shop.

In April 1969 I applied, successfully, for a post in the Exeter area manager's office as bonus clerk in the paybill section and remained there until I retired in March 1989. However, I did a number of different jobs, including preparing bonus statements, paybills and rostering of station staff – signalmen, carriage cleaners, shunters, clerical workers, supervisors, drivers, firemen, guards and, for a time, workshop and carriage and wagon workers.

Once, I also saw the Queen, when she arrived in the royal train to distribute the royal Maundy money at Exeter Cathedral. It was the first time for years that so many BTC police officers (about 70 men and women) had been at the station: they formed up on the forecourt for a photograph to be taken.

When I was on relief work I also did announcing duties at Torquay, Okehampton and Barnstaple and well remember the regular announcer at Okehampton, with his strong Devonshire accent, saying: "Okehampton, Okehampton, Okehampton; change here for Boode (Bude) and Lanson (Launceston); platform one for Boode and Lanson". I often wondered if passengers from London and the North really knew what he was saying.

So my railway career finally came to an end: mainly, most enjoyable.

On 6 October 1947 Mr Jim Kelly began work with the GWR at Heathfield Station and was to stay with the railway until 1969:–

After completing my education at Newton Abbot Grammar School, I joined the railway as the junior clerk at Heathfield Station, where my sister was the senior clerk. The vacancy had occurred there as extra clerical help was required to deal with the 'lignite' traffic from Blue Waters Mine, at Bovey Tracey, which had

Heathfield Station, where Jim Kelly began his career on the railway as a junior clerk. Waiting at the platform is 0–4–2T No. 1427 with its two-coach train bound for Newton Abbot.

Geoff Howells

been reopened as a result of the 1946/7 fuel crisis. At that time the government required industries to accept a quantity of lignite to supplement its normal coal supply, lignite being a form of soft or immature coal. An article in a January 1998 edition of the 'Mid-Devon Advertiser' reads:–

'50 years ago …

The great opencast workings of British Lignite Products Ltd., at Blue Waters Mine, Bovey Tracey, has been slowed down considerably by the continuous rain, which has turned the place into a sticky sea of a mixture of lignite and mud.'

Extra documentation was required at the station to invoice, route and record these consignments which, at their peak, involved as many as one hundred coal wagons being loaded and despatched from Heathfield in a day. In fact, Bovey became a mini-boom mining town for a while, and it was even said that certain types of young ladies, usually associated with mining boom towns, had moved into the district!

When coal production returned to normal, nobody wanted to burn lignite, which was unsatisfactory for most industries, and the boom ended as suddenly as it had begun. The end of the lignite traffic also meant that there was no further need for extra clerical assistance at Heathfield, so I was sent to Torre Station, on the then Newton Abbot to Kingswear branch line.

As with Heathfield, Torre Station, at the time, was experiencing a boom of its own. Many people were taking their first English holidays after the war years. Mass car ownership and extensive road transport was still some years away, and most people and goods were carried to the Torbay holiday area by rail. Torre Station was the parcels and goods handling depot for this trade, and as many as eight railway delivery vehicles were employed full time on deliveries to shops and hotels in the Torbay area. This required a great deal of extremely boring paper work, checking waybills, delivery sheets and dealing with the many complaints, and tracing goods which had gone astray.

A view of Torre Station on 10 May 1958 as 0–4–2T No. 1427, after taking water, pulls away with the 10.05am Paignton to Moretonhampstead train.
Peter W. Gray

Torquay Station booking office was my next posting, again quite busy issuing tickets and dealing with train enquiries. At that time the stationmaster was still wearing a Victorian frock coat and striped trousers, which designated Torquay as an important destination. It was said that he wore this for the sole purpose of meeting the then famous *Torbay Express* from Paddington. This was a world away from today's station manager, with a grey suit, plastic name tag and, of course, mobile phone.

A spell of duty followed in a railway office which few people would remember today – the Strand Railway Enquiry Office, situated opposite what was then the Pavilion Theatre. The railway was busy and important enough in 1948 to warrant a town enquiry office, and the staff there dealt with passenger enquiries, sold tickets and made seat reservations, with charts. These charts were of railway carriage seating, which we marked off, similar to the system employed in the theatre opposite to book theatre seats. This labour intensive activity was very different from today's computer system, which can provide a ticket, seat reservation and train times for the entire railway system, from the north of Scotland to Penzance.

As a young man of only sixteen, I found this type of railway work much more amenable than the hard grind of parcels and goods work at Torre. The office, situated as it was right on Torquay Harbour, with its boats and holidaymakers, was ideal for chatting up the girls who were on holiday. It was also quite common to meet and deal with show people appearing at the Pavilion. Some of these were quite famous at that time but, nevertheless, still required railway information, as even they travelled by train in 1948.

Resulting from this work, I became established as a junior relief clerk and was despatched to any station in the Newton Abbot area which required additional clerical assistance. Bovey Station, near where I now live, was one of the stations in which I did a spell of duty.

National Service in the Royal Engineers at Farnborough claimed my next two years, from age eighteen to twenty. At the time part of the National Service obligation, when released from full-time service, was to serve three years as a reservist. This entailed a compulsory camp attendance for two weeks each year. My reserve camp was the famous Royal Engineers Railway depot at Longmoor, in Hampshire, now no longer in existence. This establishment is folklore for all railway enthusiasts, but it surprises me that many other people have never even heard of it.

On my return from the army, I was again placed on the relief roster, going to various stations and depots, as before. These duties entailed rather irregular hours of work, which did not fit in with the social lifestyle of a man in his early twenties. So, when a post became vacant at the Newton Abbot locomotive superintendent's accounts office, with regular 'nine to five weekends off' duties, I transferred to this section.

Bovey Station, on the Moretonhampstead branch.

Geoff Howells

The next eight years I spent dealing with pay and locomotive costs accounts. During this time I re-met an old friend, both of us being old Newton Abbot grammarians, married her and we had our first two children.

Towards the end of the 'fifties the dreaded threat of closure and rationalisation was beginning to be felt. It was also darkly hinted that there were electronic machines, called computers, being developed that would in future perform all this tedious manual clerical work. These predictions proved to be correct, and in 1960 the office was closed down and the work centralised in offices at Swindon, themselves since closed.

From the somewhat distant and cloistered environment of an accounts office, I transferred to the factory office of the old 'Newton Abbot Carriage and Wagon Works'. The buildings were actually the original works of the South Devon Railway and had been built in 1852: many of these buildings still exist and are now occupied by private firms as part of the Brunel Industrial Estate.

After the initial shock of the change from a quiet accounts office, the noise and bustle of a railway factory office seemed to be much more a part of the actual running of the railway. Work performed in carriage and wagon repair shops was, perhaps, the most interesting of all railway repair work as it involved a number of different trades. Wood-working skills were required on the interior of coaches, while other trades comprised coach builders, wagon builders, upholsterers, glaziers and painters. Metal sections of vehicles were repaired by welders, riveters and blacksmiths, all busying away at Newton Abbot. Much of this work had remained unchanged in principle for 100 years, but in a few years all this was to be swept away, along with much of the old railway.

Newton Abbot shed yard in 1961, with the roofs of the old carriage and wagon works visible above 4–6–0 No. 4037 *The South Wales Borderers.*
Mike Vinten

At this time, 1961, the railway industry was beginning to undergo many changes. Steam was to give way to diesel and many new management and clerical procedures were to be initiated, in line with those changes. As with working practices, many old clerical procedures had not changed in principle for 100 years. The most profound change of all was on its way – the Beeching holocaust, with its massive closures and staff redundancies.

In the light of these changes, I was selected and promoted to become part of a new management and clerical structure, which was to operate in the new Newton Abbot diesel depot. This depot had been the old steam shed and repair shops, and had been converted, at huge cost, to accommodate and service the new diesel locomotives. Working and operating these new procedures was to occupy me for the next eight years, until 1969.

At this time local government was looking to such employers as the railway to provide staff who would be able to introduce into local government these updated practices. A similar post to my railway job was created by the old Newton Abbot Urban District Council (now part of Teignbridge), which I applied for and obtained. Consequently, I left the railway, after 22 years' service, in October 1969 to become a local government officer.

One interesting feature of my railway years was that I had served in four different departments, so I had experienced various types of railway work. Many of my contemporaries did not do this and so had little knowledge of how the other half lived. For example, it was possible for a booking clerk on a station to spend 40 years in say Newton Abbot booking office and never once set foot inside the locomotive shed office some 50 yards away across the lines. The shed clerks also had never set foot inside a booking office. This system tended to make staff insular, with little knowledge of, or sympathy for, the work problems of others.

When I look back on these experiences, it seems to be a world away from today's railway clerical work, with its totally integrated systems, its computers and minimal staffing.

K. R. was born in 1912 and joined the GWR in 1927:–

I became a messenger in the telegraph department at Exeter St David's Station when I left school. In those days most messages were sent and received in morse code, and a GWR code book was in general use: this meant that often one word could be used to represent half a page of instructions concerning the running of trains, rolling stock, etc.

When I was at St Thomas Exeter Station on August Bank Holiday Monday in 1932 more than 18,000 people went from there to Dawlish Warren, Dawlish and Teignmouth before lunch. Rail travel was very popular then, as few people had their own cars.

I then moved to Tiverton for family reasons and spent most of my forty years' service in that area: Tiverton was the next largest export station to Bristol in the South West. The firm of John Heathcoat & Co., makers of fine fabrics (they made Queen Elizabeth's wedding veil), regularly sent large consignments to Chicago and New York for all the big firms there, including Macey's & Marshall Field's, as well as to almost every country in Europe. The firm of EV Twose & Stenners also exported their

TIVERTON STN (OLD ROAD) 1935 — THE ONE THAT GOT AWAY

Above and below: Two of many cartoons drawn by K.R.

K.R. *(Reproduced by kind permission of Tiverton Museum)*

SERIOUS SITUATION ON THE CULM VALLEY RAILWAY

105

agricultural and sawmill machinery to Norway, Sweden and Denmark. In addition, pedigree bulls were sent to Australia and Canada from the Crazelowman breeding farm of Webber & Sons.

Life was pretty uneventful there barring the Annual Horse Show and the nearby Bampton Fair, where hundreds of Exmoor ponies were penned and sold in the main street, and gipsy families from all over the area gathered to meet their relatives and sell their goods. This usually ended up with fights in the pubs, settling old scores among the families. Little wonder the police always had a black maria nearby!

Although we were graded as porters, on branch line stations we were expected to do up to four hours a day on clerical work, for which we were paid nothing extra. Some of the best penmen I knew were porters and very proficient at station accountancy. No extra money was paid for this work, either.

At the end of the war an unexploded bomb was found in the railway bank near Hele, so all of the main line trains from Exeter were diverted up the Exe Valley line to Tiverton, and thence to Tiverton Junction. It was quite an occasion to see the 'up' and 'down' *Cornish Riviera Express* trains pass each other at Bampton! These branch lines were also very useful at other times: for example, when the heavy spring tides smashed the sea wall at Dawlish and all of the main line trains were diverted via the Teign Valley and Moretonhampstead branch lines, between Exeter and Newton Abbot. Sadly, all of these branch lines have long since been closed.

I finally left the railway in 1968, after 41 years' service, but, under the voluntary redundancy scheme, I was granted no pension and, instead, simply received a refund of my superannuation contributions. I then sat the Civil Service entrance examination, coming 32nd out of 4,900 candidates, and spent the next nine years working for the Inland Revenue until I retired at the age of 65 – with a small pension. Like Johnny Walker, I am still going strong.

(My father had worked on the railway for an even longer period of time than I. In fact, at the age of 18 he'd become a fireman at Landore, in Wales, and, not long afterwards, been loaned by the GWR to the broad-gauge Cornwall Mineral Railway, at St Blazey, as a driver. Later, he had also worked at Carn Brea, the centre of the tin and copper mining industry in Cornwall, and seen the track there converted from broad gauge to narrow gauge. Finally, he had moved to Exeter, where, as a 'Top Link' driver, he had driven the Royal Mail Travelling Post Office train every night for the following 20 years; one week to Paddington, the next to Penzance, and so on.

The terms under which he had joined the GWR stated that he would retire at 65: instead, he was given three weeks' notice to finish at 60, with a pension of 24 shillings (£1.20) per week. All the drivers of his age were treated the same way. The directors of the GWR said that they regretted it, but the economic situation made it necessary! The letter concluded 'in passing, we would like to thank you for your long and faithful service'. Afterwards an ex gratia payment of 5/– (25p) per week was made by the directors until they received their old age pension on reaching the age of 65.)

❋❋❋❋❋

9. CROSSING KEEPER

Mrs Phyllis Tarr (the widow of Arthur Maker) recalls the happy times spent living in the crossing keeper's cottage at Lowery Crossing, on the GWR branch line from Yelverton to Princetown, during the late 'thirties:–

I was brought up at Pitts Cottage in the little village of Sheepstor (situated on the south western edge of Dartmoor) and was barely 15 years old when I met Arthur. At that time he was working in the blacksmith's shop at Burrator Dam for the Plymouth Corporation and my friend dared me to speak to this rather handsome young man: little did I realise that only four years later I would become Mrs Arthur Maker! My father, incidentally, had also been employed by the Plymouth Corporation and had worked on the construction of the dam in the 1890s.

Arthur Maker, in 1934.
Mrs P. Tarr

It was in 1929 that Arthur and I married, the year in which he became a plant driver engaged on raising the level of the dam. We took a little house in Horrabridge, where Sylvia and Heather were born, but in 1937 we had the chance of moving into the level crossing cottage at Lowery, on the Great Western Railway's Yelverton to Princetown line. Mr Huggins had been the crossing keeper for the railway until then, but he and Mrs Huggins were retiring and moving out. Also, the Plymouth Corporation had bought the trackbed and taken over the cottage from the railway, and wanted to put someone into it.

Lowery Crossing, looking towards Burrator Reservoir and showing the crossing keeper's cottage to the left of the track.

W. E. Stevens (Courtesy of A. R. Kingdom)

The railway company was very good to us when we moved, even though they weren't our landlords; they even gave us wallpaper and helped with the decorating costs. The cottage had three bedrooms and was quite a size really, and all the lighting was by oil lamps. I also had an old black range to cook on. Rainwater served for the washing, but our drinking water came from the Devonport Leat, down the hill a little way. To collect it, the railway company gave us a two-wheeled cart with a covered basin on, which acted as a water scoop. Arthur and I would then have to trundle this down to the leat, scoop up a few gallons of drinking water and start the long haul back up the hill: it really was quite a weight! That water, though, was the best I've ever drunk, better than out of the taps these days.

Although Arthur kept on his plant driving job for the Plymouth Corporation, he now also took on responsibility for the level crossing. The little road down to the reservoir wasn't very busy, however, as only about four or five cars a day went through. Most of the time the gates were left open to cars: they had to be opened by hand, and with two gates on each side it was quite a job by yourself.

In those days there were about four trains a day on the Princetown line. I recall that the first was at 9 o'clock, which returned at eleven, and then there were the afternoon ones. If

109

Arthur was at work I had to be there to open the gates, and I remember that as each train approached a bell would ring in the little shed opposite the cottage, on the other side of the line (the linesmen used this shed for their meals and shelter). The train would then come through, giving a whistle as it passed. Of course, we soon got to know all the drivers on the line, and Bill Gough and Cyril Stephens, his fireman, became great favourites with our children.

Arthur's weekly wage was two pounds and the rent was five shillings (25p), so there was not a lot of spare money to be found for a family of six, Kenneth and Ivor being born whilst we were at Lowery. The nearest shops were at Yelverton village and I walked in to do my shopping twice a week for things that Arthur couldn't grow in a vegetable garden he dug a few hundred yards down the line, towards Burrator Halt. We also kept chickens down there, and I remember one day Sylvia going to collect the day's eggs: she was walking back along the line when she tripped on the sleepers and fell. All the eggs in her pockets were broken – what a mess!

Wild strawberries grew on the trackbed on the Princetown side of the crossing gates and on Sundays the children would go out and pick enough for everyone's tea; they were lovely. The Sunday trains had been stopped in the 1920s, so these days were now quiet on the line. However, there were the charabancs and day-tripper's

A view just beyond Lowery Crossing, with 2–6–2T No. 4410 and its coach on the way to Princetown.

R. C. Sambourne (Courtesy of A. R. Kingdom)

cars, perhaps as many as a dozen on some Sundays. And, children being children, because there were no trains they closed the gates to the cars: the drivers then thought that they were getting a bargain when they paid the children a penny a car to open them!

I remember that one day during the week Sylvia had walked off to Meavy School and left Heather, who was four, playing with her dolls by the line. She then came in and told me that there was a snake on her doll, so I went out and hit the thing with a broom, and killed it. I think it was Fernley Stephens, the linesman, who told me later, to my surprise, that it was an adder.

The winter times were a bit rough. Sometimes the roads were blocked with snowdrifts, but the train always got through. It had a huge plough bolted to the front of the engine when the snow blocked the line that soon did the job, but what a noise it made as it went through. Still, I never knew the train to get stuck when we were at Lowery. During these cold times dear Fernley would let us have some of the railway steam coal to burn on the range. It came in huge lumps and you had to smash it up to burn, but steam coal glowed very hot and was a welcome addition when nobody was looking!

It was the outbreak of war, in 1939, that really changed things for us. The road above and below the crossing was barricaded by the army, and cars weren't allowed through. Everyone was worried about the German invasion you see, and the dam and the trains were a good target, so the road had to be closed. Consequently, the crossing gates could be left open for the trains to go through from then on and the keeper wasn't really needed. In any case, Arthur had his 'call-up' papers and we moved away to live at Walkhampton, although I never took to living in such a crowded place and missed our little cottage by the railway line. My cousin Rosie took it over with her son after we left, but she didn't stay long and soon it was empty again.

The gates were still left open for trains after the war, and if anyone wanted to go through with a car they had to open them by themselves. Then came that sad day in 1956 – going to see the last train on the line. After that the tracks were pulled up and soon our little cottage was also demolished.

That blizzard in 1963 wouldn't have caused such problems to Princetown if only they had left the trains running; they would have got through, I'm sure. Of course, if it was open now it would be a little goldmine, but the carriages that were so full on the last day it ran were never full when it was running four times a day. There was only one carriage in those days, with a few goods trucks.

We sadly lost Arthur a few months before he was due to retire in 1971, but, to the end, he still worked for the Plymouth Corporation, down at Crownhill. We had shared some wonderful and happy times at Lowery with our young family, in our little cottage in the woods. Arthur would have loved to have seen the trains still running by today, I'm sure; such a shame!

Lowery Crossing in February 1957, with the track having been lifted but with the cottage still intact – for a little longer!

R. C. Sambourne (Courtesy of A. R. Kingdom)

(**This chapter was kindly contributed by Simon Dell, MBE of Tavistock on behalf of Mrs Tarr, who is now 88 years old. It is written as related to him on 1 October 1998.**)

❄❄❄❄❄

PASSENGER

10. PASSENGER

Mrs Grace Horseman recalls some of her many train journeys, from early childhood days:–

In the early years of the 20th century there were few small boys who did not cherish the dream of becoming an engine driver when they grew up, especially if they had access to the Great Western Railway: to them, the thought of speeding through the countryside at the controls of one of those majestic monsters, belching forth clouds of smoke and steam against the clear sky, or plunging into dark tunnels, was something magical.

Being a mere girl, I had no such ambition but, nonetheless, I was fascinated by the trains that sped along the railway at the bottom of our London garden, on their way to and from Clapham Junction.

I was only three years old when, in 1915, I accompanied my mother and two sisters (one older and the other younger) on a train journey to Winchester, where my father was already stationed with the Royal Army Service Corps. My impressions of that first journey are vague – a mixture of crowds of people, noise and smoke, and the 'clickety clack' as the wheels rolled over the rails. The following year we returned to London when there was a lull in the air raids and my father had embarkation leave: fortunately, his orders were cancelled as otherwise we might never have seen him again. Instead, he returned to Winchester with his unit, and was then sent to Bath.

He managed to find accommodation there for us, and for the first time I rode on a GWR train. By now I was nearly five and able to enjoy the luxury of taking my turn at sitting by the window, watching sheep and cattle grazing in the fields, passing distant hills or streams and rivers and grassy banks studied with primroses and other flowers. I also found how easy it was to get a smut in my eye through the open window, although my mother was careful to shut it whenever we entered a tunnel. That was frightening at first, the darkness lit only by sparks from the engine,

113

but later I quite enjoyed it.

My first impression at Bath was of arriving at the railway station there, expecting to be met by my father, and the sense of desolation when all the other passengers had disappeared and we were left alone on the platform. Eventually a porter approached us and, having checked our name, handed a message to my mother stating that my father was unable to get leave to meet us and that we were to get a cab to a certain address. Most of the luggage had been sent 'Passenger's Luggage in Advance', but I carried my doll and own small parcel. Later I was to appreciate the many majestic buildings in Bath and the joy of the surrounding countryside, especially walks by the river or over the hills.

My only brother was born in Bath, in December 1917, and soon after that my father was sent abroad to Italy, but we stayed where we were until after Armistice Day on 11 November 1918. Again, I had the joy of travelling by train to London and eventually arriving to the noise and bustle of Paddington Station, overawed by the enormous domed roof.

For the following years we had family holidays at Winchester or on the south coast, travelling on the Southern Railway; then, from 1923–29, I was at boarding school in Hertford, so became accustomed to the dirt, smell and smoke of Liverpool Street Station, on the LNER line – not a patch on the GWR, I thought. In 1931, after I had completed a course at the Triangle Secretarial College, I was invited for an interview at Bristol by the Rev. A. R. Millbourn, headmaster of Colston School, whose secretary was due to leave him shortly.

It was the first time that I had travelled to the Westcountry since 1919, so I had every reason to feel excited as the train puffed slowly out of Paddington Station, accompanied by the slow 'clickety clack' of its wheels. Then, after passing rows of houses and factories, we reached the open countryside and all the old magic returned. It was springtime and, after years in London, it was a thrill to see primroses and some early bluebells along the grassy banks.

We arrived on time at Temple Meads Station, and I saw the headmaster waiting for me (with the pre-arranged signal of a copy of 'The Times' under his arm) on the platform, at the end of a very pleasant journey. I was then at Colston School for seven years – a very happy time of my life – and went home for part of the school holidays three times a year. I never tired of the journey and each time I noticed something different. When we neared Westbury I always watched eagerly for the first sight of the 'White Horse' cut on the side of Bratton Down. In the sunshine the chalk outline was dazzling against the dark background and I wondered about the men who had created it in prehistoric times. Was it part of their pagan rituals!

I also explored many beauty spots around Bristol, but mostly with the headmaster and his wife or with members of staff, who all had cars. Occasionally, though, when one of my sisters had come to stay with me during the holidays, we explored further afield by rail – still my favourite way of travelling!

With rumours of war circulating, I decided, in 1938, that it was time to find a job in London so as to be with my parents, and obtained a post as secretary to the secretary and to the managing director of May & Baker, at their head office in St Paul's Churchyard. However, shortly before the outbreak of war I was asked to move to Dagenham, where the managing director and secretary from head office had to go to replace the former director at their works.

Once war began I found that I was being used increasingly in welfare and personnel work, as so many of the staff were being called up. Many were young men, RAF reserves, and, sadly, a number of them were to lose their lives within a few months.

The Government appreciated the need for trained personnel and welfare officers under wartime conditions, and when the opportunity arose I applied, successfully, for a place at the London School of Economics, evacuated to Cambridge. That was fine, but the journey to Cambridge turned into a nightmare as it took about six hours, by taxi, even to reach Liverpool Street Station, due to a devastating air raid on St Paul's and the surrounding area during the previous night. Then, when I did eventually reach the station, looking forward to a hot cup of tea, I found that parts of that, too, had been bombed and there was no gas or electricity, probably no water either. By that stage it was also becoming late in the day, and the outcome was that it was dark before I reached the comparative peace of life in Cambridge.

After I had qualified at Cambridge, I applied for a post as personnel assistant at W. D. & H. O. Wills at Bedminster, in Bristol. This, of course, meant attending an interview and provided me with another opportunity to travel on the GWR, from Paddington to Temple Meads Station. Furthermore, because my application for

115

A photograph of Bristol Temple Meads Station taken from the bridge by Bath Road engine shed on 1 May 1955 and showing 4-6-0 No. 1009 *County of Carmarthen* leaving on the Sunday 10.52am for Exeter.

Peter W. Gray

the job proved successful, I was able to enjoy the same journey again shortly afterwards, but, even so, it was very different travelling in wartime! Trains were dirty and very crowded, and were often late. Also, if it was night time, and there was a raid on, trains would travel very slowly, in almost complete darkness.

After a while I was asked to go to Swindon on a temporary basis, which meant more rail travel, as from time to time I would have to return to Bristol for staff meetings. On these occasions I was issued with a first class ticket and, because I had to leave Swindon very early in the morning, I had breakfast on the train; a traditional English breakfast at that, even though it was war time.

My next move was to Trowbridge, where I became personnel officer, so I was then able to enjoy travelling on the local branch lines: Bradford-on-Avon was one of my favourite spots. As there were many girls from Cornwall, who had been conscripted to do factory work, I also formed a social club and tried to provide different forms of entertainment for them. Invariably, these included short train journeys to Bath so that they could take part in netball matches, or go for rambles.

When the V1 'buzz' bombs began to fall on London I decided that I ought to return home to live with my parents, so I obtained a post as personnel officer at Allen & Hanburys, in Bethnal Green. That meant a halt to my travels to the Westcountry (apart from occasional holidays) until my husband and I retired to Bovey Tracey (Devon) in 1981. Then we mostly travelled by car, but since his death, in 1989, I have occasionally used the train again. Once I even went on one of the new Speedlink trains, with diesel engines, to Truro in order to visit my sister! But, although it was a very pretty route, I much preferred the old-fashioned individual carriages to the present day ones: they remind me of trams!

It was whilst he was living in Bristol as a young boy that Mr George Moore first became interested in trains:–

I was given a Hornby No 1 train set in the 1930s, which was added to over the years with presents at birthdays and Christmases. In fact, it grew into quite a sizeable collection, and later, when I became a teenager in the war years, I was able to sell it at a small profit: by then, production of this kind of toy had ceased, so demand was high. Prior to this, in order to play with my layout, I had to negotiate with my mother for the use of one living room for

117

LMS 2P class 4–4–0 No. 40563 of Templecombe Shed pilots SR 'Westcountry' class Pacific 4–6–2 No. 34040 *Crewkerne* with the 'down' *Pines Express* at Tyning Bridge, Radstock in the mid-1950s. To the right of Radstock East signal box, Sentinel Wagon Works 0–4–0 Tank No. 47191 shunts a line of wagons under 'Marble Arch'.

Simon P. Bowditch

a week during each school holiday and used the time available concentrating on trying to imitate the real thing.

My father's job increased this obsession with trains in my early childhood days. He was a traveller for Franklyn Davey, a tobacco firm which was a branch of the Imperial Tobacco Co and involved in producing, amongst other items, chewing tobacco used by miners. This, in turn, meant that my father would sometimes visit the area around the North Somerset coalfield and on such days, during the school holidays, he would take me with him, to Radstock. Here, the main customer was a wholesaler, whose premises were situated between the two level crossings. Consequently, after my father had parked his car and gone off to attend to his business, I was able to sit and observe the various trains that passed by on the Somerset & Dorset line, including the famous *Pines Express*. At the same time I could also see what was happening with the coal trains on the adjacent GWR branch as well as watch the two-coach stopping passenger trains (Bristol Temple Meads to Frome) and the unique GWR 'pick up' goods train, so it was a real treat.

Apart from occasional excursion trips, such as from Temple Meads to Weston-super-Mare (Locking Road), and from Bristol St

BR standard class 4–6–0 No. 75073 enters Radstock North with the 1.10pm Bath Green Park to Templecombe train on 25 August 1962.

Mike Vinten

119

Phillips to Bath Green Park (via Mangotsfield) on the LMS line, I recall one holiday in particular during the 1930s, which we spent at St Ives, in Cornwall. Here, my attention was regularly diverted from the main attraction of a holiday (the seaside) as I was more interested in the little branch railway line cut into the hill behind the beach and terminating at the nearby station (situated on the side of the same hill). Along this single line came the regular local passenger train of three coaches, hauled by a tank engine, and the daily goods train. Not only that, but during the 'middle' Saturday the scene became even more interesting with the arrival of ten-coach holiday special expresses, including the Saturdays only *Cornish Riviera Express*, from Paddington – manoeuvred along the branch by two 45XX tank engines in front and one behind to aid the movements in the station. What excitement! What joy! This was as great as that of the passengers as they poured out of the trains on to the station for the best week (or, if fortunate, two weeks) of the year.

A view overlooking the platforms of St Ives Station and Porthminster beach, with 2–6–2T No. 4549 arriving with the 2.15pm train from St Erth on 4 August 1961. In the bay platform can be seen sister engine No. 4570.

Peter W. Gray

These inspiring and nostalgic days were soon to be destroyed by the Second World War, a period when the railways were, perhaps, at their busiest, moving troops and supplies. Travel by civilians was discouraged but, of necessity, they had to use trains occasionally.

At the beginning of the 1940s my father's job moved the family home to Cardiff. Until his call-up, in June 1941, I used to accompany him up the valleys during the school holidays. What a feast awaited my eyes! The view was one of long and winding main lines, upon which was a procession of slow-moving trains, some travelling downwards with loaded coal wagons and some travelling upwards with empties to be shunted into colliery sidings to await reloading. In fact, the vast coal traffic dominated the scene, over which there was a constant film of sulphureous smoke. Intermingled with this almost continuous goods traffic was the occasional passenger train.

I also have memories of rail travel during this period. One of my mother's sisters travelled from Bristol to Cardiff during the winter of 1941. There had been a blitz on Cardiff during the previous night, causing the closure of the main line between Newport and Cardiff due to time bombs having fallen close to the track. The result was that my aunt's journey lasted for five hours as the train wound its way around the alternative valley route, thus taking three times longer than normal.

On another occasion, after her brother had been killed in October 1943, my mother decided that we should spend the following sad Christmas with my aunt and cousin in London. However, the ensuing journey took over four hours in a packed train. Not only was it impossible to pass down the corridor, due to the press of passengers, but at one stage there were also seventeen people in our compartment (seating eight)! Yes, at times it was necessary to travel and, on these occasions, people were very tolerant, kind and helpful. Furthermore, this togetherness created a friendly and kindly environment.

At the end of the 1940s I was undergoing my period of national service, and on every Sunday evening the 7.20pm train for Paddington left Bristol with not only civilian passengers but also large numbers of national servicemen returning from weekend leave. On one occasion I recall one of the famous GWR 'Hall' class locomotives struggling to pull a seventeen-coach train loaded with passengers out of the station and what a wonderful sight it was. At

121

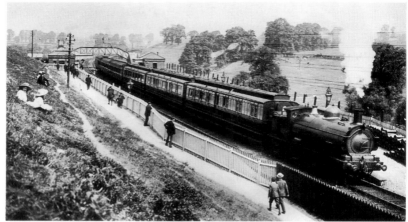

Above: A passenger train during the early part of the century, heading towards Bristol, draws to a halt at Ashley Hill Station on the steep Ashley Bank. This was before the line was quadrupled in the 1930s and housing and road development covered the background scene.

Below: A scene which shows the real meaning of the steam age. A huge output of dark sooty smoke pours into the air from a wagon fire close to the main Exeter line just south of Bristol Temple Meads Station at busy Pylle Hill goods depot.

'Memories': Corn Exchange, Bristol

the same time, it also taught me great respect for this class of locomotive and for all GWR engines for that matter.

I ended my national service being posted to a civilian firm in London, but was able to return home for the weekend on every Friday evening during the summer of 1950. I travelled (24/– (£1.20) return) to Bristol on the 6.30pm train from Paddington. On most Fridays this train ran in two parts, a regular GWR practice at busy times, and in three parts on the Friday before a bank holiday.

In the late 1950s I was regularly involved in business travel by train. Although I went, on occasions, all over the country, my main route was from Bristol to London, a journey undertaken once or twice every week. Initially, all of the trains were steam-hauled, but gradually diesels took over until steam locomotives were withdrawn completely in 1966. The changeover was not without its problems, with diesels regularly breaking down in their early days. This was frustrating, to say the least, when returning from a busy, hot, tiring day in London. One summer evening there was a diesel failure between Chippenham and Bath, where the track runs alongside the main A4 road. At the time, a double-decker bus was approaching on a run to Bath and this led to some of the railway passengers swarming across the line and to about thirty of them, many in business suits, climbing over the boundary fence and clambering aboard the bus, after it had stopped! Meanwhile, the remaining railway passengers (myself included) had to wait about half an hour until a rescue steam engine, a 'Hall', approached our train from Chippenham. This then gave rise to a big cheer and to the crew responding by smiling with delight as their engine passed the stationary coaches, with the passengers hanging out of the windows applauding their presence. Officialdom was not amused!

During this period we lived close to, and overlooking, Ashley Hill Station, in North Bristol, situated on the steep Ashley Bank. The track was then four lines. Goods trains travelling northwards from Bristol had to stop for a banker engine to help them up the steep incline. The whistle signals of the engines and heavy output of steam to move the considerable loads was music to the ear, especially at night.

The scene was enlivened during the summer as on Saturdays, in particular, there was the massive movement of the holiday passenger trains on the line: one after the other they moved down both south-bound tracks towards the city. Some were scheduled to stop at Temple Meads, while others used the St Phillips avoiding

123

line, where they stopped to change crews. Each train would be bursting with passengers, all eager to reach their holiday destinations in the South West: the list of place-names like Torbay, Newquay, St Ives and Minehead gave a vision of magic. As the trains merged with those from South Wales, London and the North East, most passengers could only hope that delays would not be too great at Taunton, the Wellington Bank or Newton Abbot, or on the twisting, up and downhill line between the latter important station and Plymouth.

In 1960 the famous Blue Pullman was introduced on the London line, and I regularly travelled on the morning business train. The 10/– (50p) supplement attracted first class attention, and a great breakfast could be enjoyed on the two-hour journey to Paddington. Old-fashioned Pullman stock was substituted on occasions when the Blue Pullman sets were withdrawn for servicing. What an interesting experience and movement back in time to another age!

The Blue Pullman was withdrawn in 1973, just before the appearance of the High Speed Trains, in 1976: these provided a great change, with a service to London in one-and-a-half hours. One train from Bristol Parkway in the morning ran non-stop to Paddington, covering the 120 miles in a mere 63 minutes. It was just about possible to finish a second cup of coffee as the train roared through Reading, at high speed!

In 1980 I retired. Rail travel then took on a new dimension as I was able to enjoy some trips with special fares for the retired. The highlights, however, were two British Rail Landcruise trips to Scotland, which covered a large area and enabled my wife and me to visit many interesting places, including Oban, Mallaig, Fort William, Isle of Mull, Iona, Kyle of Lochalsh, Inverness, Wick, John O'Groats and the Orkneys. We also travelled on the Settle to Carlisle line; all in great comfort, living on the train and being well fed and looked after by excellent, friendly staff.

When I was in my sixties I worked, for four years, as a volunteer guard on David Sheppard's East Somerset Railway at Cranmore, near Shepton Mallet. This is a re-creation of the GWR branch line set in the heyday of the steam age and is operated to a very high standard for the benefit of the interested public. While I was there I had, first of all, to be trained to BR standard and passed medically fit, and then went on to enjoy what was a great and valuable experience – only a few miles from where my interest in trains had been generated all those years earlier, at Radstock!

Now, in the late 1990s, where do the railways go from the very low state they are in post privatisation? I would hope forward. As roads become more congested, and big capital rail projects such as the Channel Tunnel unfold, the opportunities to re-exploit their great potential, not only with passenger traffic but also with freight, will unveil themselves to the benefit of us all. So, yet again, we may see busy Summer Saturdays in Devon and Cornwall, and maybe the recreating, in some form, of a few of the branch lines in the South West that were so important in their day, bringing trade and prosperity to many small country towns and seaside resorts.

The Reverend Peter Pullin's love of steam trains dates back to the early 'thirties, when he was a very young boy living in North Bristol:–

My interest in steam trains was aroused at a very young age by the sound of their hooters filling the early morning air where I lived in North Bristol; sometimes I could hear them coming from Temple Meads Station, over two miles away. In addition, when my mother took me shopping, I was first of all intrigued by what to a small boy was an awesome railway viaduct, known as 'The Arches' (this carried the line between Avonmouth, Clifton and Temple Meads over the Cheltenham Road and is, incidentally, still in use to this day). Then, much more wonderful, was the experience of actually riding on a train as we undertook the short trip from Montpelier Station to Temple Meads.

Before catching the train we would have to walk down the steps from Cromwell Road to the booking office. This, in itself, was very exciting, but when the train arrived and we piled into an isolated, third-class railway compartment, its grey seat covers decorated with what looked like chicken wire netting, that was something else. Then, just a minute or so later, and with the window having been pulled up by a heavy leather strap until it latched shut because the train would be going straight into Montpelier tunnel, there was one big hoot and we were off.

An even greater joy as a very small boy was to go from Bristol to London on *The Bristolian*. It is to the credit of Brunel's track and the steam locomotive design engineers that even in those pre-war days the *The Bristolian* covered the 117 miles (via Badminton) non-stop in 1 hour 40 minutes. This compares quite favourably with today's HST – 125s.

125

The Bristolian after having been brought into Paddington on 12 June 1959 by 'Castle' class 4–6–0 No. 5085 *Evesham Abbey.*

Peter W. Gray

On one occasion, in 1936, we were met at Paddington by an uncle who lived in Bromley, Kent, and on our way there we passed the site of the Crystal Palace, where hoses were lying across the road because it had just burnt down.

As boys before the war, my brother and I were fortunate enough to spend two or three holidays at Goodrington Sands. Our lodgings overlooked the large marshalling yard (where flats now stand) and every morning we were awoken by the sound of 'chuff, chuff, chuff, chuff, chuff, chuff – bing bong, bing bang bong, bing bong' as the tank engines shunted the loose-coupled goods wagons into their correct places.

Another wonderful thing was to see a 'King' or 'Castle' class GWR locomotive pulling *The Torbay Express* along the embankment behind Goodrington South Sands, where a few choice holiday huts occupied the site on which now stands a massive swimming and water chute complex. Happily the steam trains still run there, although only from Paignton to Kingswear.

During the Second World War, in January 1941, a small rather tearful boy stood with his mother on Stapleton Road Station waiting for the Cardiff train to take him back to his second term at boarding school in West Wales. However, once the train had arrived and was under way, tears were fairly soon forgotten in the exciting things that lay ahead, like the Severn Tunnel and stations with names like Magor and Llanfern. At Cardiff we changed and waited for the train from Paddington, which would take us through the industrial zones of Neath, Port Talbot and Swansea, to Carmarthen. Swansea High Street Station fascinated me because it was a terminus, and so we went all the way up the valley only to have the engine change ends and pull us all the way back down again.

At Carmarthen there was another wait and then the three-coach Aberystwyth train, which ran only three times a day, enabled us to complete our journey to Lampeter Station.

During my school days in Lampeter, I became more and more interested in travel and joined the 'Wycliffe Travel Bureau' (WTB), founded by our history master, Charles Taylor. The WTB organised all the end of term tickets and routes for the boys' home-going. Because of this work, I got to know the station clerk, Mr Emery, and his wife (a childless couple) who, from time to time, invited me to tea in their tiny but very cosy cottage right near the station – a bit of much-appreciated generosity and home comfort, far away from Bristol.

Two things I remember of that period are the Aberayron Railcar (one of the GWR's original push and pull combinations, comprising a locomotive and a single special coach, with a second driving position at the opposite end of the coach) and the notice by the pedestrian crossing gate – 'STOP, LOOK & LISTEN', words which have re-echoed in my mind when tempted to some hasty decision.

In the meantime, the six to eight hour journey from Bristol to Lampeter, and return, was made three times a year, and there was always the compulsive desire of a small boy to look out of the windows of the steam trains – despite the inevitable smut in the eye! After a year or so some of the other boys and I would also manufacture a home-made key, comprising a three-eighths square piece of iron, so that we could lock and unlock compartment doors! Above all else, though, I remember how much I enjoyed the journeys and how well I became acquainted with Stapleton Road Station. It does, of course, stand on top of an embankment and so affords an overall view of that crowded part of Bristol East. To one side is St Mark's Baptist Church, where my uncle had ministered some years earlier, and down the road, at that time, was a shop called 'The Paintmore Company', where a young lady worked who had cared for my brother and me occasionally, when we were younger. We sometimes popped in there for a cup of tea before catching a train.

The Beachley to Aust Ferry which marked the last leg of Peter Pullin and David Bladwell's 100-mile cycle ride in July 1944.

Peter Pullin

In July 1944, when I was aged fifteen and preparing to return home for the summer vacation, the passenger train services between Lampeter and Bristol (and elsewhere) were disrupted by the need to deliver troops and munitions to France following the D-Day landings. As a result, a companion (David Bladwell) and I decided to cycle the 100 miles over the hills and to cross the River Severn on the Beachley to Aust Ferry, there being no road bridge, of course, in those days. The outcome was that after setting out from Lampeter at 6am, we eventually reached Bristol shortly past 4pm. Meanwhile, another of my Bristol school friends left Lampeter on the train at 8am, but did not arrive home until 8pm. So, if nothing else, we proved that it wasn't 'quicker by train' – we had saved two hours!

In my last school year, 1945–6, Wycliffe College returned from its war time home at St David's College to its own premises at Stonehouse, in Gloucestershire, where the Air Ministry had been in occupation. Now we were on two main lines: the GWR from London to Gloucester and the LMS from Bristol to Gloucester. There was also a branch line which extended from the LMS station

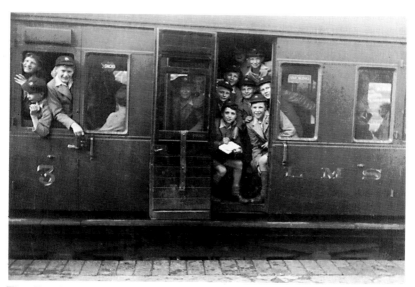

The 'Beetle Squasher', with some of the boys of Ryeford Hall using the Stonehouse to Nailsworth train on the occasion of its final run before the closure of the line in June 1947.

Peter Pullin

up the Stroud Valley and on which ran one or two coaches and a tank engine: this train was affectionately known as the 'Beetle Squasher' and passed by the junior school that I had attended, at Ryeford Hall.

As my family moved to London at this time, it was the GWR line through Kemble and Didcot which became my new route home from school. I loved clocking the train's speed with the wayside mileposts – I still do it, although it is more difficult in an HST.

On arrival in London as a seventeen year old, I had my first experiences of the LNER – also known locally as the 'Late Never Early Railway'. Brown commuter carriages were pulled by engines facing out to the home counties, but they returned to London with the tank engine at the other end, yet still facing the same way, ie coal box first.

A year or so later, as a young naval rating, I enjoyed the delights of Pullman travel! The first train out of Southampton Central after the beginning of a weekend leave was the 5.20pm – and it was all Pullman. Moreover, for a two shilling (10p) surcharge on top of my forces cheap ticket, I could sample the comfort of a reserved seat, a table with a lamp and tea which was served. We were whisked off

129

to Waterloo in one and a half hours by a 'Merchant Navy' class loco, I suspect. This was much more romantic than the multiple-unit electric trains from Portsmouth.

I love steam trains, and steam locos, but I can understand their demise. Some years later I was living in Manchester and occasionally went home to London for weekends, using British Railway Midland Region. The journey was scheduled for about four hours, or slightly less, for the 180-odd miles, but we were invariably late at Euston, often taking $4^1/2$ hours even though the train was sometimes double-headed. Whether this was due to the quality of the coal or the exhaustion of the firemen, I would not know. However, I shall never forget the Friday evening when the steam locomotive(s) was replaced by a single Type 4 (?) diesel-electric loco and we romped down to London in under $3^1/2$ hours – but that was no higher an average than for *The Bristolian*.

I am impressed by the smooth acceleration of the modern electric High Speed Trains and by all the technology behind them, but who amongst those born in the 'twenties or 'thirties can forget the haunting sound of the wheels at speed on non-welded rails going a diddly-dee, a diddly-dee, a duddly-dee, a diddly-dee, etc. Aaaah!

Ms Betty Travis, who now lives in Plymouth, remembers the pre-Beeching days when she appreciated the opportunity to travel on the GWR in Somerset:–

When my family moved to Clevedon, in Somerset, during the Second World War I enjoyed visiting the local railway station. It was at the far end of a single track, and trains shunted back and forth on the leisurely four-mile journey between Clevedon and Yatton Junction.

Although Clevedon had such a small station it still boasted a liberal display of posters, which fired my youthful imagination. I longed to be with the small children enjoying donkey rides on the sands, but they were always on the far side of the country. Other advertisements whetted my appetite as I gazed at young boys, caps askew, licking their lips over Fry's chocolate cream bars. Then there were a couple of grinning waifs, known as the Bisto kids, who intrigued me, but mostly I admired the infuriatingly pretty little girl depicting the apparent wonders of Pear's soap. All these posters made my waiting time enjoyable.

The station staff seemed terribly old, but strangely they did not retire for another thirty years! The stationmaster was always popular, perhaps because of his willingness to delay the train for a few minutes if any of the regular passengers had not arrived.

When I was only five years old my invalid mother wanted me to travel to Yatton with a message. She insisted that I was old enough to travel alone, so although I felt nervous and timid I walked to the station, bought my ticket and waited to hear the steam train approaching the buffers. There were two main carriages, with individual compartments opening directly onto the platform. The steps were high and I wondered if I would be able to climb them, but a kindly countrywoman stretched out her hand to help me.

The rhythm of the engine was soothing, but I disliked the smuts which flew in through the open window and stung my eyes. Nevertheless, the journey was unhurried and I enjoyed looking at the country meadows full of spring flowers. There was even time to glimpse the occasional cowslip and, to my delight, lambs skipping in the fields. At the half-way mark I recognised the old stone tower of Kenn church.

Alighting at Yatton was easy, as I jumped down the steps onto the side platform. This was adjacent to the main platform, where express trains roared past en route to Temple Meads, frightening me with the sudden rush of speed. On the far side of the railway bridge was a further side platform where trains left for Wells.

I liked Yatton Station from that day onwards. It was clean and there were waiting rooms on both sides of the line. In winter, I could warm my hands by the coke fires in the waiting rooms: in summer the flower beds were a source of delight with their scented wallflowers and neatly planted polyanthus. Yatton was definitely a well-tended station.

Occasionally my mother and I took a day trip to Wells, but the journey was incredibly slow as the train stopped at the tiniest halts. Sometimes we also went on day trips to Weston-super-Mare. As the train from Clevedon was likely to be delayed by the kindly stationmaster, this meant a mad dash over the railway bridge to catch the fast train to Weston. This train fascinated me as it had a corridor and, as day trips were popular at the end of war time, was generally overcrowded with trippers and hordes of excited children with buckets and spades. Luggage was an additional hazard in the corridor at weekends, but I enjoyed the general air of anticipation.

Over the years I frequently visited Yatton en route to my home in Clevedon and was thankful for the rail link, as it meant that I could avoid the hassle of two difficult bus journeys. Eventually, though, it all came to an end when Dr Beeching did a grave disservice to the community of North Somerset by axing not only the rail link to Wells but also the invaluable connection with Clevedon.

0–4–2T No. 1463 standing in the bay platform at Yatton Station with the 1.03pm train to Clevedon on 31 October 1959.

Peter W. Gray

✳✳✳✳✳

11. RELIGION

An important part of the railway background is the British Transport Christian Fellowship. Below are details supplied by Mr Bob Gray, the editor of the BTCF News:–

The British Transport Christian Fellowship (formerly the Railway Service Christian Union) was established on 6 November 1926 by a small group of Christian railwaymen employed by the four major railway companies of that period – the London Midland & Scottish (LMS), London & North Eastern (LNER), Great Western (GWR) and the Southern Railway (SR). Among the founder members was Cecil J. Allen, a well known author on railway engineering, who later served as President of the Fellowship. The present membership consists principally of railway people, serving and retired, who assent to the principles which motivated the founders. All members must subscribe to the Basis of Faith which is 'The acceptance of the Holy Scriptures in their entirety as being the Word of God and the only basis for Christian faith and practice. Personal trust in the Lord Jesus Christ and His atoning sacrifice as the only ground of Salvation'.

The object of the BTCF is to advance the Christian faith and to promote fellowship among those employed by British Rail and allied undertakings. It forms a special link between individual Christians and encourages the establishment of local witnessing groups at places of work. There are branches at a number of the larger railway centres, but in some cases members find themselves as the only Christian witness in their office or workshop – to such the BTCF is an invaluable link.

A *News* is published three times a year on the activities of branches and members, together with other items of topical interest both spiritual and industrial. Every issue contains an evangelistic item with an invitation that helpful Christian literature is available free of charge on request. The Fellowship has a vision of outreach and two attractive tracts with a 'railway' theme have been written by our president, Jack Heap. These are entitled *The*

Permanent Way and *Journey through Life* – another is being prayerfully prepared. These are available to anyone requesting them. A supply has been donated to the London City Mission for the use of their missionaries called to work among railway personnel.

An annual conference featuring Bible teaching ministry is held at a Christian centre over a long weekend, and a rally to celebrate the Fellowship's birthday used to be held on a Friday evening in London. This, however, was replaced a few years ago by an annual Fellowship Day at an interesting venue, and we have since had enjoyable days at Richmond, St Albans, Gloucester, Rochester and Coventry. The days are very informal, but arrangements are made for folk to meet at a local church for a short time of devotional worship and tea before dispersing.

The Fellowship is very conscious that despite having taken advantage of advertising in the House Journal *Rail News* there are probably some active (and retired) Christian railway people who have never heard of our existence. To anyone reading this article and who is interested in knowing more about the BTCF, they are invited to write for further information to:–

> The Hon. Gen. Secretary,
> Paul Chow,
> 12 Lichfield Way,
> Selsdon,
> Croydon
> Surrey
> CR2 8SD

Mr Colin Walker first became interested in railways when he enjoyed train spotting at Reading Station. Later, in 1963, he joined the railway as a mathematician in operational research, ending his career at Paddington. He is an enthusiastic member of the British Transport Christian Fellowship, his faith having meant much to him for many years, and he contributed his story to their *News*. It was as follows:–

My parents were God-fearing, if somewhat formal Methodist folk, and I value my Christian upbringing. I spent my early years at Caversham and South Reading.

I came to God traumatically and it happened as a result of my father's death when I was eleven. He died quite suddenly from a stroke: it was all over in a few minutes. Neither my brother nor I was at home, which protected us both from the obvious trauma. As it happened, it was the first time I had ever been away from my parents, for I was at a Crusader House Party on the Isle of Wight.

The news was broken to me by Jack Watford, the General Secretary of the Crusaders Union, who happened to be the Leader of the holiday. Walking round the beautiful grounds of Bembridge School, he spoke gracious words of comfort, and prayed with me. As I sank to my knees that night beside my bed, I just cried, "I believe – Help!" Although you could call it a child's conversion, later on it sunk in that Jesus was real, and in God's provision, as I realised, I had been in the best possible surroundings for receiving this blow, the Crusaders playing a major part in my discipleship as a teenager. But those early days were hard at school and I found it quite a stigma to have only one parent, when all my friends had two.

My interest in railways started young, with train spotting on Reading Station. I remember my father getting me past the ticket checks on what was Platform 4, using his London season ticket. I well remember *Gossington Hall*, with its slightly unusual smoke box number plate, as one of his regular commuting train engines. My first taste of a railway job was while I was still a student, as a Christmas night extra at Reading, and in vacations at Paddington 'Parcels To Be Called For' office, on Platform 12. That was in 1959–62.

From Cambridge University I entered the railway proper in 1963 as a mathematician in operational research. This was at Blandford House, Marylebone (now demolished!), participating in the '222' Christian Fellowship with "Plum" Warner and, later on, Jack Heap and Ray Brown as leaders. After a move into freight, and two years at Euston House, I was catapulted back to Marylebone, administering the 'Forward Freight System' at headquarters. I well recall Harvey Vinall from Euston sending his computer input to us in his wonderful copperplate handwriting! After thirteen years at '222', re-organisation and promotions brought me to Melton House, Watford, and to CU Group. In fact, edible products manager was my last job before the Speedlink closure in 1991, with that difficult withdrawal from wagonload services and the traumatic effects on staff and customers alike.

Funnily enough I have less recollection of my last two working

135

years – in Railfreight Distribution at Enterprise House, Paddington – than the others. This is because I had to retire sick in September 1993, having contracted encephalitis, a viral brain infection which left me in a semi-comatose state for nearly two years. But my recovery since then has been truly miraculous, and the Lord has been a faithful God. I now reckon about 90% of my mental faculties are back (some would say 90% of zero is still zero!). Like Job, the Lord has in a real way given me more than I had before in terms of a changed outlook and opportunities for unpaid volunteer work; also identification with brain-damaged folk like epileptics, with whom I can relate and work closely. My exciting last project has been a rail escort service, using my travel facilities, to take disabled folk on holiday or home to parents. Fortunately my memory weaknesses do not extend overmuch to railway geography, which has firmly stuck with me. Names and faces are not so easy, but fortunately I have a computer for the BTCF conference work!

Since starting to type these words over this week, I have had rather a rude shock, 'the sudden end' of one of my volunteer jobs! Life is full of surprises, isn't it! This seems to be God's way of keeping us on our toes.

To conclude, I am reminded of that well-known hymn verse, which I can re-echo as my own experience:–

'Through all the changing scenes of life,
In trouble and in joy
The praises of my God will still
My heart and tongue employ.'

The Reverend David Hardy has been a railway enthusiast since his early childhood days, so it was appropriate that he should extend this interest as a Methodist Minister by becoming a part-time railway chaplain, a position that has brought him much joy:–

It is interesting how many clergymen are keen on railways! I have always been fascinated to know why this should be so, and particularly like the story of one bishop who, when asked why he was a railway enthusiast, is supposed to have replied: "Well it is just nice to see something move that I have not had to push!" Perhaps one of the most famous clergymen with a railway interest was the late Rev Wilbert Awdrey, the author of the *Thomas the Tank Engine* stories, who said that "For all their faults, railways and the church are both the safest ways of reaching your destination!"

My own interest in railways began, like so many, when I was a boy, growing up in Exeter. Our family home was in St Thomas, within sight and sound of the former GW main line. I used to go 'trainspotting' and still have my old notebooks. In my teens and early twenties, however, the pressures of study meant no time for trains.

My interest rekindled in 1969 after I had acquired my qualifications in science. However, a career in science was not to be, as I believed that God was calling me to become a Methodist Minister. Eventually I was accepted and studied at Cambridge from 1972–74. Our studies finished at the end of June and as I could not take up my first appointment until September I had to fill eight weeks. This I did by working for British Railways at the civil engineers' depot at Chesterton Junction. For two weeks I humped sleepers about etc – and realised how unfit I was! Then, real bliss, I was asked to learn the job of yard checker in order to cover whilst the regular man went on his annual holiday. This was wonderful! I sat in the shunters' hut drinking tea, labelled wagons, recorded all that was entering or leaving the yard, rode on engines and took photos. And, I got paid for it! We still have the three-piece suite that I bought with my earnings, although by now that is getting a bit the worse for wear!

A Cambridge steam crane re-railing a wagon at Chesterton Junction when David Hardy was employed there as a yard checker during the summer of 1974.

Rev. D. Hardy

137

"I just happened to be at York Station!" when this steam special departed for Harrogate, via Leeds, on 10 May 1980.

Rev. D. Hardy

I went into a circuit near York, where I was Minister to four churches. What better place for a railway enthusiast – especially as many of my congregations worked for the railway and fed me with all sorts of useful information, for example about steam specials! In addition to my 'normal' church work, I found myself having what is known as an 'Industrial Chaplaincy'. This meant visiting a bottle-making factory in the name of the churches (all such chaplaincies are ecumenical). I enjoyed it very much. It is good to be able to spend time with non-church people and to seek to show the love of Jesus. Such a chaplaincy is of a pastoral nature. Although I would wear my 'dog collar' so that people would know what I am (I found that they do not like swearing in front of a 'vicar'!), I would never initiate a conversation about religion. I would only talk about my faith if they asked me questions. At first I was amazed how, on every visit, people would ask me something about matters of faith, even if they were not churchgoers. I began to realise that it is not surprising really. I believe that everyone is seeking for meaning in their lives. My conviction is that God has made us in such a way that we cannot find our true selves unless we are in fellowship with Him. This harmony with God, I believe, is possible for everyone as we open ourselves to God's love, as he has revealed Himself to us supremely in Jesus Christ.

We were near York from 1974 to 1980, and then we moved to

Nuneaton, in the Birmingham Methodist District. I had no industrial chaplaincy there – and I missed it! I decided that it would be a good idea to talk with the 'District Full Time Industrial Chaplain'. Amongst his responsibilities was British Rail. I asked if he would like an 'assistant' and, after having the permission of my churches and the railway authorities, and the agreement of the unions, I began visiting the stations, signal boxes and depots in the area. Again, it was a pastoral ministry and I made a lot of very good friends, drank numerous cups of tea – and took loads of photos over the eight years that we were there. I am still in contact with many of the men that I was privileged to meet. A couple of years ago I went back to speak at the Nuneaton Railway Circle. I showed dozens of slides and shared some experiences of my work as chaplain in the area. Afterwards the secretary wrote in the local paper: "The meeting thought that they were in heaven and had a hell of a time when Rev David Hardy came and talked of his work as a Railway Chaplain!" One great joy for me was to find that one of the signalmen whom I knew had become a committed Christian. He told me of the wonderful difference finding Christ had made to his life.

In 1988 we moved to Newton Abbot and I transferred my railway chaplaincy to cover what was then the Exeter area of British Railways. Over the years since then I have got to know a great many really interesting people – and taken many more photos!

My chaplaincy on the railways is mainly concerned with pastoral work – both for the employees and retired staff of the companies of the former British Rail and, since 1996, when we moved to Totnes, the volunteers and staff of the privately-owned South Devon Railway. I visit folk who are sick or in need and have taken a number of funerals for railway people.

My chaplaincy comes under the auspices of the Railway Mission, an organisation set up in 1881 to bring the Gospel to railway workers. The Railway Mission is non-denominational and has a number of full-time chaplains around the country and also a number of part-timers, like myself. We offer to provide literature, Gospels and a calendar. If I am fortunate, I have one of my photos in it. I am also supported by the Home Mission Department of the Methodist Church, who pay my expenses. It is a policy that we are never paid by the organisation that we serve.

I enjoy so much talking to railway folk and hearing the stories of life on the railway. You will gather how interesting this can be from contributions to this book. I also enjoy the sense of humour that railway people often have, and many times get my leg pulled about working only on Sundays – and, no doubt, getting double time for it! On one occasion I was doing an interview for Radio Devon's 1–2–1. This is a religious magazine programme broadcast on a Sunday. They had got to hear of my chaplaincy and sent a reporter, complete with tape recorder, to the station to interview me and some of the people whom I visited. One of the men interviewed, since retired, was really enjoying telling the keen young reporter of my work. As he could see the reporter was very earnest, he thought that he would have a joke with him. "Yes", said my friend, "our chaplain does a wonderful job! In fact, he has converted me!" The reporter's eyes lit up, thinking he was on to a good story. "Yes", repeated my friend, "he has converted me from beer to lager!" Fortunately for me, being a tee-total Methodist, they edited that bit out before broadcasting it!

In addition to the pastoral side there have been a number of special services and events. I very much enjoy going to the railway pensioners' tea, which is held in Exeter each year. There are usually about 200 folk there, and if you were to add up the combined years of service it must run into thousands. You can

A group of retired signalmen enjoying themselves at the railway pensioners' tea at St George's Hall, Exeter on 29 April 1997.

Rev. D. Hardy

imagine the stories and the fun as they reminisce with each other! On one occasion I was able to arrange with the management for my Chairman of District (a sort of equivalent to a bishop in the Church of England) to have a cab ride on a High Speed Train from Exeter to London. As he is a railway enthusiast himself (yes, another one!), he loved it! I guess that it will have done my promotion prospects the world of good!!

1997 marked the 150th Anniversary of the coming of the railway to Totnes and the 125th Anniversary of the opening of the branch line from Totnes to Buckfastleigh and Ashburton, and so an exhibition on the history and current work of the Railway Mission, along with special services and events of celebration, were organised at Totnes Methodist Church throughout the summer.

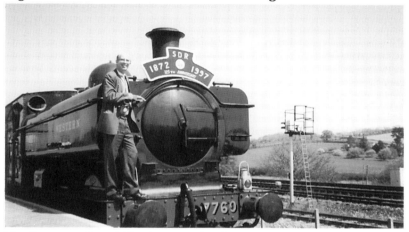

The Reverend David Hardy poses for the camera on the buffer beam of 0–6–0PT No. 7760 at Littlehempston Station (Totnes) during the 125th Anniversary of the opening of the branch line from Totnes to Buckfastleigh and Ashburton celebrations on 1 May 1997.

Karen Lang

Steam train trips are arranged on the South Devon Railway on two evenings in December each year for carol singing. In 1997 a total of £800 was raised and shared between NCH Action for Children and the Methodist Church in The Gambia. I am fortunate that the treasurer of our Methodist Church at Buckfastleigh, Mrs Jill Elliott, is the wife of the general manager. She, and one of the employees, Mark Ireland, who is the organist at Ipplepen Methodist Church, do all the organising. Mark rigs up a public address system and plays his keyboard for the carols. We serve

141

coffee and mince pies in the train.

I have also organised annual Railway Mission 'Songs of Praise' services which were held at the Avenue Methodist and United Reformed Church in Newton Abbot and, for the last two years, at the Methodist Church here in Totnes. They are ecumenical services, and friends from Anglican, Baptist and Brethren Churches have all been involved in leading them with me: music is provided by the The City of Exeter Railway Band (formerly The Exeter Area British Rail Band) and is excellent. The work of the Railway Mission locally and my chaplaincy were featured in 'Wild About Devon' on Westcountry TV in the autumn of 1997. This is the one and only time that I have been on TV.

It is an honour for me to have the privilege of visiting the railway people and their families. For me it is a wonderful way of combining work and pleasure! I enjoy taking photos and now have quite a collection, not only of engines, signals and the like but also of the people I have got to know and love. I only wish that I had more time so that I could do more, but I do have to work in the Methodist Churches of Totnes and area as well – and not just on Sundays either!

Len Lucas, railway chaplain at Kings Cross, gives details of the Culross Mission:–

Culross Mission was founded in 1897 to minister to the spiritual and practical needs of railway staff and their families and to provide assistance in times of need. Culross Hall was erected in 1890 by the Great Northern Railway Company as part of Culross Buildings, a block of forty flats for railwaymen and their families, and was officially opened in 1897 by the former Lord Colville of Culross KT, chairman of the GNR. These buildings are situated at the back of Kings Cross Station.

The London City Mission appointed Mr K. Mitchell to be the missionary/chaplain in charge of the Mission Centre. He was supported by a committee of railwaymen presided over by Sir Henry Oakley, a director of the GNR. From those days to the present time the missionary/chaplains were seconded to the railway free from any imbursements from the various railway companies.

During 1984 Culross Hall and Building were closed down in order for proposed development/redevelopment of the Kings

Cross area. As a result of this the missionary/chaplain was relocated to a room in the West Side Offices of the station where the work of Culross Mission continues among railway staff and their families.

The ministry of the chaplain was twofold:

1. To present the Gospel of Salvation through the Lord Jesus Christ to all who would be prepared to listen; and
2. to offer comfort, counselling and practical help to any railway employees and their families regardless of status, race or religion.

This continues to be the aim and the ministry of the chaplain today. Many railway staff and families have cause to be thankful for the spirituality and practical help of the chaplains over the past 100 years – Messrs K. Mitchel, J. W. Kirby, G. Holland and A. Cook.

The support for practical needs has come (and still comes) from collections and donations by railway staff, including retired staff and many interested friends from all around the country. The Mission is happy to receive donations at any time, with the assurance that the gifts that are given are used completely for the purpose for which they are given. There are no administrative costs.

As the present chaplain I am here at your service to offer any comfort or help in practical and spiritual ways. Please feel free to call in at the office or phone and I will do my best to help you. It is good to talk. As well as Kings Cross railway companies, I also cover Thameslink. The postal address is 47 Carew Road, Tottenham, London N17 9BA, and the office is at 113 West Side Offices, Kings Cross Station. The phone number is 0171–314–4106 (internal 00–54106).

12. A GLIMPSE OF THE 19TH CENTURY

Mrs Grace Horseman gives a brief description of one of the earliest 'railways' to be constructed in the South West and explains how, in effect, new generations are 'growing up' on it:–

Canals preceded railways as an economic way of transporting heavy goods from one place to another, and in 1790 James Templer began construction of the Stover Canal, in Devon. Starting at Whitelake (a deepened tidal leat at Newton Abbot), this canal, originally, was to have gone as far as Bovey Tracey, with a branch to Chudleigh, so that large deposits of ball clay in those areas could be transported direct to the port of Teignmouth, via the Teign estuary. For financial reasons, however, only some two miles of the canal were ever completed, and when it was opened, in 1792, in terminated at Ventiford, near Teigngrace. Nevertheless, its aims were achieved with remarkable success, as soon there were up to seventeen barges (seven owned by Templer) operating on the canal, each carrying between 25 and 35 tons of ball clay to Teignmouth. From thence it was transported in sea-going vessels to Liverpool to serve the Staffordshire pottery manufacturers.

On the death of James Templer in 1813, his son, George, inherited the family estate and it was he who built the Haytor Granite Tramway in 1820. Prior to then, granite was already being extracted from Dartmoor, where the tors bore witness to its presence, but it had to be carried laboriously by horse and cart. And it was this fact, combined with a contract being received for the supply of granite for use in the construction of London Bridge, that persuaded George Templer to proceed with the construction of the tramway – to link up with the Stover Canal.

The peculiarity of the line was the material used for its construction – granite! This, however, was due to it being so readily available in the area, whereas iron was much more difficult to come by – and expensive. So, roughly hewn blocks formed the

144

rails, which varied in length from about four to eight feet and were about a foot square in section. These were merely placed in line with one another, without being joined, although the ends were dressed sufficiently to make a tolerably good fit between one block and the next. In addition, on the running surface, the blocks were cut to form a flange, about three inches deep and about seven inches from the inner edge, the gauge between these flanges being four feet three inches.

Because the tramway served more than one quarry on Haytor Down, its total length, including secondary routes (for which points were constructed using grooved stones and metal cheek-pieces mounted on rotating pegs), was some ten miles. Of this, the journey from the main quarry to the Stover Canal at Ventiford accounted for about eight miles, and it was on this section that the line fell away by more than 1,200 feet. Mostly the descent was gradual but, at times, the horses, which pulled up to a dozen loaded, flat-topped wagons (each about 13 feet in length) were used as a brake by their handlers, or a long pole dragging on the two-feet diameter iron wheels of the wagons sufficed. Otherwise, the route presented no problems whatsoever as it had been so well planned that apart from one short cutting on the open moor there was neither cutting nor embankment for the whole distance.

The quantities of what was particularly high quality granite carried over the tramway initially amounted to several thousand tons per annum. Much of it was sent to London, not only for use in the construction of London Bridge but also for such buildings as the National Gallery, The Old General Post Office, Covent Market Garden and the British Museum. However, as time wore on the business began to suffer from outside competition and staffing inefficiencies, with the result that by 1858 the tramway had fallen into disuse and the quarries become deserted. Gone by then, too, were the quarrymen and their families who had 'grown up' there, for many of them had lived in cottages built of quarried stone on Haytor Down.

In 1862 the lower section of the tramway, from the southern outskirts of Bovey Tracey to Ventiford, was purchased by the directors of the then newly incorporated Moretonhampstead & South Devon Railway Company to form part of the route of their proposed broad-gauge line from Newton Abbot. As a result, when the line was subsequently constructed, between 1863 and 1866, that part of the tramway (except for minor deviations) became totally

145

obliterated. Over the years that followed other sections of the tramway were also lost, to either agriculture or development, but beyond Bovey Tracey much of it remains to this day. Furthermore, since 1975 Haytor Down has been in the ownership of the Dartmoor National Park Authority, and the main length of the tramway upon it designated an Ancient Monument. More recently, in 1984, the Amenities and Countryside Committee, the Dartmoor National Park Committee of Devon County Council, and the Sport and Leisure Committee of Teignbridge District Council gave approval to the preparation of a joint study of how the route and the remains of the Haytor Granite Tramway and the Stover Canal could best be conserved, as well as to afford opportunities for public access and recreational use. This, in turn, led to the creation of the 'Templer Way' – a walking route of some 15 miles following as closely as possible the line of the Haytor Granite Tramway, the Stover Canal and the Teign estuary, between Haytor and the sea at Shaldon.

Nowadays, the 'Templer Way' is a popular attraction to both visitors and locals alike, particularly the section of the granite tramway on open moorland, so, in effect, new generations are now 'growing up' on it.

A short section of the granite tramway on Haytor Down, as photographed in 1998. Behind the spoil tip to the left of the picture is the dis-used main quarry, while above it the well-known Haytor Rocks dominate the skyline.

Karen Lang

Cecil Torr (1857 – 1928) was brought up in and near London, receiving his early education at home from a private tutor before attending Harrow from 1872 to 1876 and then moving on to Trinity College, Cambridge, where he did well as a mathematician.

Later, after having travelled abroad extensively (from the age of ten) and written a number of books and essays, he took up residence at Wreyland in the parish of Lustleigh in Devonshire and immersed himself in the history of his own locality; one of the main fruits of this was his well-known book *Small Talk at Wreyland* (first published in 1918 by Cambridge University Press), and from which the following paragraphs, primarily about the railway line between Newton Abbot and Moretonhampstead, have been extracted by kind permission of Forest Publishing:–

The existing railway from Newton to Moreton was projected in 1858, and was carried out under the Moretonhampstead and South Devon Railway Act, 1862 ... Work was begun on 10 August 1863, but not near here (Lustleigh) till 9 November. In the autumn of 1864 surveys were made for an extension of the line from Moreton to Chagford; but nothing ever came of that. The line was opened to Moreton on 4 July 1866.

Financially the railway was a failure. There was a capital of £105,000 in shares and £35,000 in debentures, but the expenditure was £155,000. And the company was amalgamated with the South Devon company on 1 July 1872, the £105,000 in shares being exchanged for £52,500 in ordinary stock, and the £35,000 in debentures for £35,000 in debenture stock. And then the South Devon company was amalgamated with the Great Western company on 1 February 1876, each £100 of South Devon ordinary stock being exchanged for £65 of Great Western ordinary stock, and each £100 of South Devon debenture stock for £100 of Great Western 5% debenture stock. Thus £100 in shares came down to £32.10s.0d. in stock; but part of the loss was wiped out afterwards, when Great Western stocks went up, £32.10s.0d. of the ordinary stock selling for nearly £60, while £100 of the 5% debenture stock sold for nearly £200.

The navvies made things unpleasant here, while the line was building. My grandfather writes to my father on 17 November 1864: "More than a hundred discharged on Monday, and a pretty

A train for Moretonhampstead at Lustleigh Station in 1912, headed by a 3101 class 2–6–2T, No. 2197. It was around this time that Cecil Torr began to write *Small Talk* from his nearby home.

Chapman & Son (Courtesy of A. R. Kingdom)

row there was: drunk altogether, and fighting altogether, except one couple fought in the meadows for an hour and got badly served, I hear. The same night the villains stole all poor old *****'s fowls. He had them under lock and key, but they broke in and took the whole, young and old … . There is not a fowl or egg to be got hearabout." …

Now that the cuttings and embankments are all overgrown and covered with verdure, one can hardly realise how hideous it all looked, when they were raw and glaring. In that respect this was the worst piece of the line, as there are four cuttings here in less than a mile, and embankments almost all the way between them. But some of the viaducts and bridges are worthy of all praise. Just below here the line crosses and re-crosses the Wrey at a height of rather more than forty feet above the stream, first on a viaduct of two arches and then on a viaduct of three. And these are built of granite, and so well proportioned, that there would be many pictures of them, could they be transferred to Italy and attributed to Roman or Etruscan builders. A little further up there is a splendid archway, where the road goes underneath the line before ascending Caseleigh hill.

The line was intended to curve round the outer slope of

Caseleigh hill instead of cutting through it; but the curve was condemned as dangerous on so steep a gradient. And the plans were altered, to the disadvantage of the scenery, and also of the shareholders, as the cuttings were very costly.

The old people here would often speak of London as though it stood upon a hill. And they could give a reason: "Folk always tell of going *up* to London." When the railway came, it was perplexing. This portion of the line ascends about 400 feet in about six miles, with gradients of as much as 1 in 40. Yet up trains went down, and down trains up.

Lustleigh station once had a signal-post, though it now has none. Seeing both arms lowered for trains to come both ways, I felt a little uneasy, there being only a single line. But the station-master said: "Well, there isn't an engine up at Moreton; and, if a truck did run away, it wouldn't stop because the signal was against it." Trucks do sometimes run away, but have never yet done serious damage.

This line was laid with the old broad-gauge rails on longitudinal sleepers, and was converted into narrow-gauge in 1892 by bringing the off-side rails and sleepers in towards the near-side. It has all

The last broad-gauge train to pass Teignmouth, on 21 May 1892.

Douglas Croker

been re-laid now with the usual narrow-gauge rails and transverse sleepers, excepting a few sidings.

On the broad-gauge there were eight seats in a compartment, first class, the narrow-gauge having only six. And in the Great Western carriages there was often a partition with a sliding door, making a sub-compartment on each side, each with two seats facing forward and two facing back. Passengers' luggage used to be carried on the roofs of the carriages, being strapped down securely and covered with tarpaulins. But this was not peculiar to the broad-gauge. I remember it on narrow-gauge lines as well, especially the Great Northern.

Some of the old broad-gauge engines were worth seeing. On the Bristol & Exeter line there were engines that had a pair of driving-wheels nine feet in diameter, and four pairs of carrying-wheels set on two bogies fore and aft. These engines were taken over by the Great Western on the amalgamation of the companies; but the Great Western, I believe, had no engines of its own with driving-wheels of more than eight feet, except the Hurricane, whose driving-wheels were ten feet in diameter. I used to hear it said that Brunel had driven the Hurricane himself, and made her run a hundred miles an hour; and these Bristol & Exeter engines certainly ran more than eighty. It was one of these that came to grief at Long Ashton on 27 July 1876. She turned right over, and threw up her driving-wheels to such a height that they cleared the train, and came down upon the line behind it ....

My grandfather did not travel in a train until 5 December 1846, and then he writes:– "I had not much inclination to go in it after reading of so many collisions and accidents, but now I think I could form a resolution to go anywhere in it; but I shall not do so, unless it is for special purposes.... I admit there is danger in all conveyances; but this, I think, with proper caution is by far the safest, and I shall in future (if ever I travel again) take about the middle carriage, for I see the hinder carriages are liable to be run into – therefore the danger is almost equal to that of the front, except the bursting of the engine."

In a letter of 13 February 1852, he warns my father of another danger: "I do hope you will leave the train at Exeter, when you come down, and not risk going on to Newton. The post is now arrived, near 3 o'clock: another landslip just as the mail train came up. This has been the fifth slip." And really the dangers were considerable then. They were reduced, as years went on; but he never got quite reconciled to trains. When eighty years old and tired of life, he writes to my father, 8 June 1869: "However glad I should be to receive my call, I would prefer home to a railway carriage."...

On 19 March my father started from Piccadilly in the Defiance coach at half past four, stopped at Andover for supper and at Ilminster for breakfast, and reached Exeter at half past ten. Allowing for stops, this meant travelling about ten miles an hour all the way, the distance being about 170 miles. He went on by coach to Chudleigh and drove from there, arriving here at half past one, twenty-one hours after leaving London. This was the last time that he came down all the way by road.

On 10 October 1842 he started from Paddington by the mail train at 8.55pm, reached Taunton at 2.55am, and came on by the mail coach, stopping at Exeter from 6.15 to 7.00, and reaching Chudleigh at 8.00; and he was here soon after 9.00, "being only $12^1/_4$ hours from London to Wreyland." Coming by the same train on 20 March 1845, he reached Exeter at 4.05 by rail instead of 6.15 by coach, and he was here soon after 7.00. On 8 August 1846 he came from Paddington to Exeter by the express train in only $4^1/_2$ hours, 9.45am to 2.15pm. He came by rail as far as Teignmouth on 26 November 1846, and as far as Newton on 2 April 1847. But the line from Exeter to Newton did not much improve the journey, as it added twenty miles by rail, and saved only seven miles by road.

He notes on 7 October 1847: "Went from Dawlish to Teignmouth by railway on the atmospheric plan, and to Newton by Locomotive." Brunel was the engineer of the line, and he had come round to the opinion that locomotives were wrong in principle – there was needless wear and tear and loss of power with engines dragging themselves along: the engine should be stationary, and the power transmitted. And he induced the company to build the line with stationary engines, which pumped the air out from a pipe between the metals, and thus drew the train along by suction. But the leakage was so great that the system was abandoned.

Coming down by the Defiance coach the fare from London to Exeter was £3 for a seat inside, and by some of the other coaches it was £3.10s.0d. When the railway had reached Taunton, the fare was £2.18s.0d. for first class on the train and inside on the coach. After it reached Exeter, the fare was £2.4s.6d., first class, and £2.10s.0d. by the express. It now is £1.8s.6d., first class by any train.

Later in his book, Cecil Torr comments about how his grandfather took his time from the station clock (at Lustleigh), and how the trains 'proclaimed the hours'. He also comments about the engines and their lack of effective brakes (c1866):–

Time seemed to be of very little value when I first knew the place. After the railway had been made (1866) my grandfather took his time from the station clock – he could see the hands with his big telescope, looking over from a stile near here. Till then he took it from the sun-dial: he writes to my father, 16 January 1853, "My watch has taken to lose lately: unfortunately the sun does not give me an opportunity to see about the time … I shall depend on my own time as soon as the sun will give it me." Though the sun gave him his time, he allowed for the equation; but many of the people here ignored the difference between mean time and solar time. The equation varies from fourteen minutes one way to sixteen minutes the other; and a variation of only half an hour was hardly worth considering in a sleepy place like this. He writes on 14 January 1851, "My watch kept stopping and brought me late to meals, and I had the frowns of the folks: so returned to the old one, which is sure to bring me home in time, as it gains a half-hour in a day."

After the railway came, the trains proclaimed the hours, as most people knew the time-tables approximately, calling the 8.19 the 8, the 11.37 the 12, etc. – odd minutes did not count. As the trains upon this branch were 'mixed', partly passenger and partly goods, there generally was some shunting to be done; but this caused no delay, as the time-tables allowed for it. If there was no shunting, the train just waited at the station till the specified time was up. The driver of the evening train would often give displays of hooting with the engine whistle while he was stopping here, and would stay on over time if the owls were answering back.

The engines on this branch were quite unequal to their work, and there were no effective brakes then. Coming down the incline here, trains often passed the station; and passengers had to walk from where their train had stopped. My grandfather writes to my father, 12 March 1867, "On Saturday we had a runaway on the rails. The train passed here at 4 o'clock with two carriages two trucks and a van, and could not get on further than Sandick road, so unhooked the trucks, and was not careful to secure them, and they went off and passed the station full 40 miles an hour. I was at the stile when they passed. Luckily did no harm and stopped at Teigngrace, and the engine came back and fetched them." I once saw a goods train stopping at the station here, most of it upon the level, but the tail end not clear of the incline; and as soon as couplings were undone for shunting, the tail end started off with all the other trucks that were behind the couplings. It is a single line, and up and down trains pass at Bovey; and the runaway ran past there. Luckily, no train was coming up.

Grace Horseman: Cecil Torr's remarks are of particular interest to me, as my bungalow is situated less than 100 yards from the site of the former Brimley Halt, on the $12^1/_4$-mile long Newton Abbot to Moretonhampstead line. The last train had long since passed when my late husband and I moved here in 1981, but the trackbed and adjoining cutting were still there, rampant with wildlife and a haven for birds and animals – and for young boys who clambered down the embankment to trespass and gather blackberries. Sadly, it is now part of the new Bovey bypass.

Our neighbour, Gerry Lott, had lived here much longer and would tell us stories of the driver who would stop the train anywhere along the route to Moretonhampstead in order to allow passengers, who so wished, to get out and pick primroses along the embankments. Then he would collect them on the return journey: the good old days!

Postscript

Although the line from Newton Abbot to Moretonhampstead was closed to passengers in 1959, it remained open for freight traffic to Moretonhampstead until 1964 and as far as Bovey until 1970. Furthermore, the section from Newton Abbot to Heathfield has remained open to this day, having been used, until quite recently, for ball clay traffic and also to serve an oil-distribution depot built on the nearby Heathfield Industrial Estate in 1966. In addition, this surviving part of the line has been used, on occasions, to stable the Royal Train, and on 9 March 1983 HRH The Princess of Wales (Princess Diana, whose tragic death in 1997 was mourned by the whole nation) even travelled by train to Heathfield when visiting Bovey Tracey. Other people, too, have had opportunities to travel on the line as part of various Railtour excursions, one of the most recent having been that organised in

Above: Brimley Halt, on the Newton Abbot to Moretonhampstead line, as it was on 31 January 1959.

Eric R. Shepherd

Below: The same view nowadays. Even the adjoining road over-bridge has been replaced!

Mike Lang

conjunction with the 125th Anniversary of the opening of the branch line from Totnes to Buckfastleigh and Ashburton celebrations, in 1997 – using an InterCity 125, no less!

The Great Western Trains Company liveried HST/C3 (InterCity 125) photographed at Heathfield Station on 26 April 1997, along with some of its many passengers participating in the 125th Anniversary of the opening of the line from Totnes to Buckfastleigh and Ashburton celebrations. Earlier the train, organised by Hertfordshire Railtours, had travelled down from Paddington to Buckfastleigh, bringing some 450 passengers to visit the area, and it was now about to undertake the journey back to Buckfastleigh, via Newton Abbot and Totnes, to pick them up once more, prior to making the return journey to Paddington.

Karen Lang

❋❋❋❋❋

BIBLIOGRAPHY

BODY, Geoffrey, *Railways of the Western Region*. Patrick Stephens Ltd 1983

BOOKER, Frank, *The Great Western Railway – A New History*. David & Charles 1977

BRITISH RAILWAY, WESTERN REGION, *British Rail's Western Region Western at Work Series No. 1*. British Railway (Western/Avon – Anglia) 1981

ESAU, Mike, *The Southern, Then & Now*. Ian Allan Ltd 1996

EVANS, M. C., *The Haytor Granite Tramway and Stover Canal*. David & Charles 1977

GARDNER, W. J., *Cleaner to Controller (Reminiscences of the GWR at Taunton)*. The Oakwood Press 1994

GREGORY, R. H., *The South Devon Railway*. The Oakwood Press 1982

HARRIS, Helen, *The Haytor Granite Tramway and Stover Canal*. Peninsula Press Ltd 1994

JENKINS, S. C. & POMROY, L. J., *The Moretonhampstead and South Devon Railway*. The Oakwood Press 1989

KAY, Peter, *The Teign Valley Line*. Wild Swan Publications Ltd 1996

NOCK, O. S., *History of the Great Western Railway – Volume Three: 1923–1947*. Ian Allan Ltd 1967

RICE, Iain – editor, *Newton Abbot – 150 Years a Railway Town*. Hawkshill Publishing 1996

SEMMENS, P. W. B., *The Heyday of GWR Train Services*. David & Charles 1990

St JOHN THOMAS, David, *A Regional History of the Railways of Great Britain – Volume 1: The West Country*. David & Charles 1981

TORR, Cecil, *Small Talk at Wreyland*. Forest Publishing 1996

WATERS, Laurence, *GWR – Then and Now*. Ian Allan Ltd 1994

LIST OF CONTRIBUTORS

Bill Batten, Exeter, Devon *(Chapter 2)*

Joyce Bond, Bickleigh, Tiverton, Devon *(Chapter 8)*

Alec Bowditch, Taunton, Somerset *(Chapter 8)*

Douglas Croker, Witney, Oxfordshire *(Chapter 8)*

David Evans, Heathfield, Devon *(Chapter 6)*

Graham Freestone, Exeter, Devon *(Chapter 8)*

Bob Gray (Editor of BTCF News) *(Chapter 11)*

Rev. David Hardy, Totnes, Devon *(Chapter 11)*

Grace Horseman, Brimley, Bovey Tracey, Devon *(Chapters 10 & 12)*

Fred Kearley, Exeter, Devon *(Chapter 4)*

Jim Kelly, Hennock, Bovey Tracey, Devon *(Chapter 8)*

Leslie King, Felixstowe, Suffolk *(Chapter 8)*

Len Lucas, Kings Cross Station, London *(Chapter 11)*

Geoffrey Mallett, Tiverton, Devon *(Chapter 1)*

Ken Mapp, Exeter, Devon *(Chapter 5)*

George Moore, Bristol, Avon *(Chapter 10)*

157

Pat ... *(Chapter 7)*

Bernard Price, Exeter, Devon *(Chapter 6)*

Colin Pulleyblank, Newton Abbot, Devon *(Chapter 3)*

Rev. Peter Pullin, Aylesbeare, Exeter, Devon *(Chapter 10)*

K. R., Tiverton, Devon *(Chapter 8)*

Reginald Salter, Taunton, Somerset *(Chapter 3)*

David Shillito, C Eng MI Mech E B Sc Hons., Ashbourne, Derbyshire *(Chapter 1)*

Phyllis Tarr, Tavistock, Devon *(Chapter 9)*

Betty Travis, Plymouth, Devon *(Chapter 10)*

Mike Vinten, Totnes, Devon *(Chapter 2)*

Colin Walker, Chalfont St Giles, Buckinghamshire *(Chapter 11)*

❀❀❀❀❀

Other Titles
in the same series:–

Growing up between 1900 and 1920
Grace Horseman
(£9.99)

Growing up in the Twenties
Jane Madders and Grace Horseman
(£8.95)

Growing up in the Thirties
Grace Horseman
(£8.99)

Growing up in the Forties
Grace Horseman
(£10.95)

Available (post free) from:

**Mrs Grace Horseman
3 Ashburton Road
Brimley, Bovey Tracey
Devon TQ13 9BZ
Telephone 01626 832300**

Other Titles available from ARK Publications (Railways):–

The Yelverton to Princetown Railway
(Anthony R. Kingdom)

The Bombing of Newton Abbot Station
(Anthony R. Kingdom)

The Heathfield to Exeter (Teign Valley) Railway
(Lawrence W. Pomroy)

The Plymouth Tavistock and Launceston Railway
(Anthony R. Kingdom)

The Totnes to Ashburton Railway (and The Totnes Quay Line)
(Anthony R. Kingdom)

The Plymouth to Yealmpton Railway (The South Hams Light Railway)
(Anthony R. Kingdom)

The Plymouth to Turnchapel Railway (and The Cattewater Goods Line)
(Anthony R. Kingdom)

The Plymouth & Dartmoor Railway and The Lee Moor Tramway
(Eric R. Shepherd)

A Winter Remembered (Events recalling the winter of 1962/63 and its effect on the railways of Dartmoor)
(Robert E. Trevelyan)